ROUTLEDGE LIBRARY EDITIONS: INDUSTRIAL RELATIONS

Volume 26

THE MANAGER'S GUIDE TO INDUSTRIAL RELATIONS

T0313027

THE MANAGER'S GUIDE TO INDUSTRIAL RELATIONS

L.F. NEAL
AND
ANDREW ROBERTSON

Routledge
Taylor & Francis Group

LONDON AND NEW YORK

First published in 1968 by George Allen & Unwin Ltd

This edition first published in 2025
by Routledge
4 Park Square, Milton Park, Abingdon, Oxon OX14 4RN

and by Routledge
605 Third Avenue, New York, NY 10158

Routledge is an imprint of the Taylor & Francis Group, an informa business

British Library Cataloguing in Publication Data
A catalogue record for this book is available from the British Library

ISBN: 978-1-032-81770-5 (Set)
ISBN: 978-1-032-84906-5 (Volume 26) (hbk)
ISBN: 978-1-032-84909-6 (Volume 26) (pbk)
ISBN: 978-1-003-51559-3 (Volume 26) (ebk)

DOI: 10.4324/9781003515593

Publisher's Note
The publisher has gone to great lengths to ensure the quality of this reprint but points out that some imperfections in the original copies may be apparent.

Disclaimer
The publisher has made every effort to trace copyright holders and would welcome correspondence from those they have been unable to trace.

L. F. NEAL

M.A.(Cantab.)

Member, British Railways Board
Formerly Deputy Employee Relations Adviser, Esso Petroleum Company
Labour Adviser, Esso Europe Inc.

ANDREW ROBERTSON

B.Sc.(Econ.)

National Institute of Economic and Social Research
Senior Research Fellow, University of Sussex
Formerly British Institute of Management

THE MANAGER'S GUIDE
TO INDUSTRIAL RELATIONS

London

GEORGE ALLEN & UNWIN LTD

RUSKIN HOUSE · MUSEUM STREET

PRINTED IN GREAT BRITAIN
in 11 on 12 pt. Baskerville type
BY T. & A. CONSTABLE LTD
EDINBURGH

CONTENTS

CHAPTER I

THE EVOLUTION OF MODERN MANAGEMENT

INDUSTRY, and therefore industrial management, seen in the perspective of history, are new phenomena. Therefore we must not be unduly surprised if they still present us with problems to which we have yet to find satisfactory solutions.

The so-called industrial revolutions which transformed the economies of nations that had hitherto known only agriculture, trade and handicrafts, aided by simple machines, brought quite new dangers and difficulties into society. They were, in the first place, something of a disruptive force, strengthening as they did the trend away from a master-and-man relationship based on custom and hardly at all on cash. Eventually, as production units grew in size, employers found themselves faced not only with all the now familiar problems of organization and control, but with the additional task of maintaining harmony between themselves, their appointed or sub-contracted deputies, and the workers.

Economic historians have pointed out that large concentrations of workpeople under one roof were not unknown in Elizabethan England, citing the celebrated example of the master clothier, William Stumpe. He may have had as many as a thousand employees, even before the discipline exerted by machinery powered from one source compelled his successors in the textile industry to congregate with their workpeople on particular sites, determined first by the location of water power, later for a variety of other reasons connected with fuel, raw materials and transport. One thing that never seemed to exert a pull over industry, but was itself pulled, was labour. The examination of labour migration in England during the early years of industrialization has been sufficient to support the belief that the people went to the factories, not the factories to the centres of population. And while this may seem both obvious and superfluous, it is not irrelevant when looking at the evolution of management and industrial relations in Britain. The attitudes that developed and hardened then inevitably conditioned the thinking of both sides.

There can be little doubt that the organizational energy of the early entrepreneurs was directed more towards the efficient conduct of their businesses in terms of profit than towards any social purpose, with the exception of men like Robert Owen, and even the arguments he used to convince his fellow factory owners that happy workpeople are more productive had to be linked with the balance sheet and not with ethics. The multitude of problems that the early capitalist had to contend with, including the raising of adequate capital, were acute, even at times producing situations that he could only solve in a paternalistic manner. For example, the scarcity of small coin in late eighteenth-century England led to the striking of tokens by employers, with which to pay their workers, and to the issuing of promissory notes and the setting up of company shops at which they could be exchanged for goods. All such activities are open to abuse, and it is the spectacular misuse of the paper promise and the 'tommy shop' that have come down to us in the literature. Not that one would deny the necessity for the Truck Acts. Equally, however, there were employers who took their responsibilities as employers at least as seriously as the squire had at one time taken his rural communal obligations.

Like the squire, however, the large employer was naturally inclined to regard his workpeople as inferior beings in many respects and therefore as in need of guidance and lacking in discipline. The early factory owner exerted strict control over his employees, to the extent of locking them in their place of work, fining them for breaches of regulations and even condoning the use of violence by overseers. If, as some economic historians have argued, the main purpose of bringing workpeople together before powered machinery necessitated it was discipline, once they had been so organized a new policy of control needed to be evolved. An easy way out for the entrepreneur was to sub-contract the supplying of labour to the overseers, leaving it to them to recruit, control and reward the people. This relieved the factory owner of all the burdens of being an employer, though it did not relieve him of social responsibility, as the subsequent Factory Acts were to demonstrate.

While the State, then, had to intervene gradually to protect the factory worker from the consequences of irresponsibility, because it could be seen that eventually it was injurious to the common good, it was also called in to protect the employers from the spontaneous defensive actions of the workers themselves. Not that the factory women and children in the textile trades, for whom the Factory Acts were brought into being, could or did lift a finger in their own defence. But simultaneously, as Chapter IV briefly describes, there had been emerging a kind of labour organization among the skilled craftsmen, who were outside the factory system, but menaced by both machinery and the apparent indifference of their employers.

Descriptions of the 'cottage industries' in the textile trades illustrate clearly the relationship that evolved between the merchant who 'put out' the work and the workers who converted the raw materials into finished cloth. The entrepreneur, the forerunner of the modern merchant converter, possessed the necessary capital, or could borrow it, and had the connections to acquire raw materials, wait for it to be spun and woven into cloth, and then sell it at a profit. He had no factory, only a straggling group of skilled families upon whom he would call to deliver, collect or to pay. Even the equipment with which they worked was his, and was leased from him. The difference between this relationship and that which eventually prevailed in the factory was that it was infinitely more casual. If the merchant did not need the labour of his cottage workers, he simply stayed away. If they had no supplementary means of support, such as a smallholding, they starved. But it was not a dramatic shut-down of a factory or a lock-out of labour.

Once the people were collected in the factory, however, it had to be a different story. Indeed, in order to have on hand the labour force that was vital to his operations the factory owner might even have to build accommodation near the works. This put him increasingly in a paternalistic situation. Whole neighbourhoods became dependent upon his factory unit. When it prospered the owners, the workers and the local shopkeepers prospered. When it ran into difficulties the repercussions were widely felt. Even when there was more than one factory in a district it was likely that they were in the same industry, or stage of the industry, as with the spinning towns, the weaving towns and the finishing towns in Lancashire, and the same general reaction to trading conditions could be expected. This was the external aspect of factory growth, and was not much thought about at the time. The damage inflicted upon communities by mining, the use of coal and of chemicals has left obvious traces. The relics of the internal conflict, as it became, are less obvious. They tend to emerge in men's attitudes and prejudices.

In his *Genesis of Modern Management*,[1] Sidney Pollard points out that it is not true to say that there were numerous precedents for the control and supervision of labour in large numbers on one site. The eighteenth-century factory owners of Britain were not the first men to have hundreds of workers under their control, but few had undertaken what they did, which was to bring together people, workplace, machines, raw material and power, and act as merchant for the product. All that the masters inherited from the past was a tradition of obedience from apprentices, and that quickly vanished as skill declined, except in certain industries, and the dependence of outworkers who were accustomed to expect work and pay from them. When their firms grew and the types of labour within them became increasingly varied, they found themselves with new problems of supervision.

As Pollard says, 'Problems which are easily soluble in a workshop became major difficulties in a factory'. The proprietor of the business, accustomed to know his workpeople by name, loses touch with them, or at least fails to make touch with newcomers. And if these newcomers are needed for their possession of new skills they are likely to be even more of an enigma for the employer. When the firm has become too large for one man to run, the proprietor finds it necessary to hand over some of his duties to an intermediate class of employee, supervisors or managers.

The use of managers was not a new departure in British business, the joint stock trading companies having, of necessity, employed them to act for the owners of the stock, but, from Adam Smith onwards, fears were expressed that such men, not having a personal interest in the company, might not exercise the close control and vigilance that a proprietor naturally

[1] London, 1965, p. 7 *et seq.*

would. By the nineteenth century, however, as Pollard demonstrates, companies had grown so large that it was inevitable that managerial functions had to be entrusted to men who were neither owners nor shareholders, but in effect a superior class of employee whose loyalties were to the proprietors.

The eighteenth century had seen the emergence of large landed estates, most of them run by agents and employing wage labour, and the rudimentary technology of the age had spurred on the opening of sizeable collieries and ironworks as well as textile mills. There was, therefore, a growing experience of delegation of authority by owners to agents. And it was bound to introduce a changed relationship between the proprietorial family and the workpeople, between whom the management stratum intruded. The traditional relationship could hardly survive in these circumstances, and the traditional methods of control were weakened accordingly. Without realizing it, the proprietors of companies which had grown to this extent had created a need for new techniques of industrial control, both of operations and men. And while the first might be forthcoming in various primitive forms under the influence of men who had engineering or book-keeping knowledge that they had gained on the job, the second tended to rely on less relevant precedents, dependent on attitudes and customs that were rapidly disappearing.

A difficulty that became apparent to the proprietors of large businesses was the tendency on the part of their managers or supervisors, where it was to their profit, to reduce payment for work done, sometimes blatantly, and at others by the over-strict enforcement of rules, the object being to make the results appear better or to put some money in their own pockets. The wrath that was publicly vented upon the proprietorial classes was frequently earned by, but seldom visited upon, their appointed agents. In sum, the situation that began to prevail between employers and employed may be described in the one word 'impersonal'.

This divorce of masters from men may be paralleled, but less dramatically perhaps, in the widening gap between ownership and management in business. As soon as the capital requirements of a company reached the dimensions of a railway project's financial needs, it was necessary to borrow widely. Before the Companies Act of 1862 and the permitting of limited liability, Acts of Parliament had to be passed to empower companies to incorporate themselves as a joint stock company (limited liability had been made illegal after the financial crisis of the South Sea Bubble). But one way or the other, nineteenth-century business displayed the dual characteristics that we take for granted in a modern company: a management element that may or may not have an interest in its results, and shareholders who play little or no part in the running of it.

It became increasingly difficult, as a consequence of these parallel developments, for owners and workers to have any direct understanding of each other's behaviour. The managers on the spot would be carrying out the instructions of a Board of Directors theoretically instructed by remote and numerous shareholders. The workpeople would be attracted to the employment mainly by the prospect of earning money and not through the family custom that father, son and grandson had always worked for this or that proprietorial family, or for similar motives.

A factor to be considered in addition to these is the undoubted acceptance on all sides that working conditions in industry were inevitably bad, that work was bound to be hard and unpleasant by its very nature. This attitude tended to be coupled with an ingrained conviction that people of working stock were inured to these hardships anyway, sometimes modified by a disinclination to believe that such hardships were as bad as they were made out to be. There have, of course, been sharp differences of opinion among economic historians as to the social evils of child labour, for example. One argument that ran counter to the standard Christian ethical condemnation of it being that it was traditional among rural families, and that they constituted the majority of the factory-working population in the early days.

The philosopher of the factory system, Dr Andrew Ure, saw nothing wrong in the employment of small children, still less women, and went as far as to observe that their displays of energy after a day's work indicated that their labours did not seem to be at all harmful to them physically.[1] Furthermore, he did not find that 'persons past the age of puberty' could be converted by training from agricultural or craft pursuits into useful factory hands. Their 'listless or restive habits' and their

[1] *Philosophy of Manufactures*, 1835.

'refractory tempers' accustomed as they had been to 'irregular paroxysms of diligence', made such adults unsuitable material to fit into the factory system, dependent as it was on regularity and the need to subordinate human weakness to mechanical strength. Dr Ure pointed out how easy it was for a child to superintend the self-regulating machinery of the new factories, thus achieving the required harmony, while more mature operatives might, under the persuasion of 'artful demagogues', combine against their masters, commit atrocities and even use the generous wages paid to them to finance further rebellion.[1]

The unquestioning subservience and obedience of the child was thus preferable to the individuality of the adult worker, with his prejudices, his standards acquired elsewhere and his tendency to combine into trade unions, especially under the confined circumstances of factory life. In the factory, people were more closely associated than ever before, and out of this association there grew eventually the organizations that gave them strength to bargain with the employers (see Chapter IV). But the whole idea of workpeople standing up for themselves to argue about pay and conditions ran counter to tradition. To many masters it seemed disloyal, even treacherous, and they did not hesitate to punish such insubordination.

Added to this feeling among the employing class that the workers ought to accept the pay and conditions that their wise and generous masters had seen fit to provide, was the firmly rooted Protestant ethic by means of which thoughtful men came to regard work almost as an end in itself. The connection between ascetic, Puritanical thinking and the capitalist outlook has been amply demonstrated by Weber and Tawney, and to practical, modern managers it must seem a remote and intolerant set of attitudes. But its influence was strong in the minds of the eighteenth- and nineteenth-century industrialists and coloured much of their behaviour and their utterances. They preached the 'economic virtues', as Tawney had called them, inculcated them into their children and hoped to convince the working class of their merits too. The high moral tone that we associate in our minds with Victorian England derives directly from these influences. It was without doubt accepted and even preached by the more prosperous and intelligent sections of the working classes, but such people were not to be

[1] Cf. E. P. Thompson, *The Making of the English Working Class*, 1963, pp. 359–61.

found employed regularly in the factories. They were usually craftsmen working on maintaining the machines or in some similar capacity, not bound to the inexorable and demanding discipline of the long working day.

This superior artisan class would have tended to develop the same outlook as the supervisors, a reflection of the paternalistic puritanical mentality of the majority of employers, but without its profound, rational basis. None the less it would have tended to make such men impatient with the importunate demands of the less skilled workers for better pay or improved conditions.

In the early years of industrialization in England economists had produced some convincing and convenient theories to explain the inevitability of the rewards of labour. The famous wages fund theory argued that the proportion of output that could be spared for paying the workers had been shown to be constant. Therefore it was useless to attempt to increase that share, because that would deplete the other shares and upset the economic balance. Senior's incredible contention that profit was earned in the last hour of the working day was another convenient belief, for it served to delay the shortening of the working day for some time. Lassalle's iron law of wages held that no matter what gains workpeople might make, sooner or later the general level of wages was bound to return to its 'natural' height.

The weight of informed opinion was thus heavily behind the employer in his endeavours to get the most from his workers. Tradition demanded their loyalty and obedience; religion and ethics demonstrated the value of hard work and the relative unimportance of material gain; while the new science of economics showed clearly how hopeless it was to fight against the natural order. Of course, being poorly educated, many workers were unable to understand or follow these arguments. Some of those who could refused to believe them but were ill-equipped to argue the other way. Thus there opened up an apparently unbridgeable gap in the thinking of the two sides of industry.

Employers and employed became remote from each other in a number of ways; intellectually and in outlook they were far apart; their working and living conditions gradually becoming those of Disraeli's Two Nations; finally there grew between them a third group wielding the authority of the employer and proprietor, employees like the workers yet of a different social class and with different loyalties, the professional advisers and the managers.

Gang leaders, overlookers, butties and other kinds of supervisor were well known and notorious for their callousness and grasping behaviour. The new professionals were quite different: better educated and therefore better mannered, more intelligent and therefore better equipped to see the advantages of a less repressive factory discipline. It was they and the enlightened employers who pursued such impractical matters as factory education, under the spur of the Factory Acts, and even a touch of welfare here and there like the introduction into the Courtauld factory of free meals for child workers and a nursery for the babies of women workers. Courtaulds were probably the first company to appoint a woman welfare supervisor.

But such charitable developments were both rare and unlikely to win much regard from a working class which was becoming less downtrodden with the effect that factory legislation and trade union bargaining had on restraining the excesses of the employer. It was also realized the 'good works' were not unconnected with religious evangelism and a superior moral tone which some employers tried hard to inculcate into their workers. As far as the employers and their loyal managers were concerned, most workers displayed an unfortunate irresponsibility of mind that prevented them from thinking ahead and therefore being thrifty, provident and sober. According to published opinion they squandered their earnings on drink, ate more than was good for them (Ure was convinced of this) and begrudged the effort of labour. Hence the detailed, strict codes of conduct and disciplinary sets of rules displayed in every factory and mill, with prohibitions on swearing, unruly behaviour, whistling and singing, idling, unpunctuality and all the familiar misdemeanours.

It was important under these circumstances to appoint and develop a class of manager with suitably moral characteristics, possessing the loyalties and ambitions that the workers conspicuously lacked. Probably the first operation with which the proprietor required help was keeping the accounts, though many preferred to keep their own as long as they could for fear of carelessness and dishonesty. It was in the counting-house, however, that the first specialists will most likely have appeared in manufacturing industry, but more in the nature of clerks

B

than professional accountants, whose origins are credited to Scotland, where they were an adjunct to the courts dealing with the estates of those judged unfit to manage their own affairs. It was in Scotland that the first accountants' associations began.

The true professional as we know and acknowledge him, qualified after service and examination, was not part of the factory population for a long time, but the empirically trained book-keeper, works engineer and general manager were. Often, naturally, they were relatives of the proprietorial family, if not members of it and, as such, bound together more closely in loyalties and interests than if they were retained merely on the strength of their qualifications. Much as the modern manager may despise nepotism, a little imagination only is needed to appreciate the advantages of having about you as proprietor reasonably efficient relations and in-laws. To persuade a valuable senior employee into marrying your daughter was one way of tying him to the firm before the days of top-hat pension schemes and share options. In short, it was important for the employer to be sure of his immediate subordinates.

As Sidney Pollard observes, in the competitive conditions of nineteenth-century capitalism, employees looked upon their bosses 'as enemies within the distributive system of a capitalist economy'. The employers were by no means unaware of this, and looked upon their appointed deputies as allies. These were inauspicious beginnings for management-labour relations.

CHAPTER II

MANAGEMENT AND LABOUR

In nineteenth-century Britain the management function was part, and a minor part, of the duties of any entrepreneur. That does not mean that he did not have to 'manage', only that he was more concerned with the immediate demands on his time made by technical considerations. In all the textbooks on the history of management theory mention is made of Boulton and Watt and their Soho factory in Birmingham. These two, respectively businessman and engineer, were mainly preoccupied in making and selling steam engines. It was only when this fast-growing business necessitated their frequent and prolonged absence from the works that they began to consider the need to establish some system of control that would function whether they were there or not.

This need to leave a trained subordinate in charge was the beginning of delegation of authority. The training, of course, would have been largely technical and not managerial, because what managing was done was empirical and bore little resemblance to the fourfold activity outlined by Brech: planning, control, co-ordination and motivation. But the kind of men to whom Matthew Boulton and James Watt would have entrusted their business had developed, as Urwick says, 'the mental tools of the scientist—definition, analysis, measurement, experiment and proof'.[1]

Men with this mental equipment, or habit of mind, practical men people would have called them, began to enter industry and trade in increasing numbers as the size of enterprises grew, though it was not until well on into the nineteenth century in Britain that a separate group of managers emerged in sufficient numbers to be identifiable, and it is not surprising therefore

[1] *Principles and Practice of Management*, 1963, p. 13. *The Pattern of Management*, 1956, p. 7.

that systematic thinking about management belongs largely to our century. In his outline history of management literature, Brech chooses Garcke and Fells *Factory Accounting* as the first attempt to bring together on paper the work of engineer and accountant, and this book did not appear till 1887.[1]

The work of Garcke and Fells differed from much earlier manuals like those of James Montgomery on the cotton industry and the much more important work of Charles Babbage, *On the Economy of Machinery and Manufactures*, both of whom published in the 1830s, in not being generalized but being intended for practical application. Hence the heavy emphasis on accounting, as with F. G. Burton's *Commercial Management of Engineering Works* (1899). For while Babbage's text is regarded as a pioneer work in management principles, actually anticipating some of the ideas of F. W. Taylor in his *Principles of Scientific Management* (1911), and while it contains much generalized thinking about the running of factories, it is not written as a specific aid to management. Montgomery, in a much narrower field, concentrates on the technicalities and related commercial activities of cotton spinning. By the middle of the nineteenth century every industry had its quota of helpful manuals. It was later that studies of techniques like accounting began to be produced for general application.

It is perhaps misleading to concentrate attention on the available literature as a means of tracing the development of management thinking. There were also articles in the contemporary technical periodicals, some of which were later published in book form. And there was the manner in which companies were run as another indication of the state of the managerial art. In *The Making of Scientific Management* there are two chapters on scientific management in practice, each dealing with one company: the first with Boulton and Watt, the second with Hans Renold Ltd., better known nowadays as Renold Chains.[2]

The Boulton and Watt example, recorded from original documents by Professor (now Sir) Eric Roll in 1930, shows a variety of rudimentary managerial ideas, from plant layout, as we would call it today, to incentive payments in the form of bonuses for the output of particular parts such as cylinders. But there seem to have been no contemporary parallels, or at least none appears

---

[1] *Op. cit.*, p. 83. There is here a long bibliography of early management writing.
[2] Urwick and Brech, Vol. II, Chapters III and XI.

to have been recorded. It seems that full, systematic control of production was hardly practised before the beginning of the twentieth century, and not a great deal even then until after 1945.

We are concerned here especially with attitudes towards labour. Boulton and Watt were deaing with a new class of labour, most of which they were compelled to train themselves, and if little or nothing appears in their documents to suggest that they had given much thought to labour relations, the explanation may simply be that they concentrated mainly on the technical and financial aspects of their business because their workers presented them with comparatively few problems.

They and their competitors, who proliferated after 1800 when the steam engine patents expired, seem to have belonged to one of two schools of thought as regards the behaviour of workpeople. On the one hand stood the traditionalists who regarded labourers as universally irresponsible and troublesome, requiring discipline and close supervision, if not some form of moral re-education as well. On the other hand there was a small group of more enlightened employers, of whom Robert Owen was probably the best known (but unfortunately he has tended to leave behind the impression of being a little eccentric) who took the humanitarian view that they should treat their workers at least as well as they treated their machines. This does not sound particularly kindly nor generous, but in the setting of the time it was denounced as unnecessary and wasteful. Hence the preoccupation in the literature with engineering and account keeping, with scarcely a mention of people.

The contrast between these two attitudes has been set out in our own time by Professor Douglas McGregor as Theory X and Theory Y.[1] Theory X is the traditional view and rests upon three interlocking assumptions: that the average human being has an inherent dislike of work and will avoid it if he can; that because of this most people have to be coerced and even threatened with punishment to get them to make adequate efforts; and that the average human being, unambitious and irresponsible but needing security, prefers to be directed.

The more sophisticated or enlightened Theory Y has twice as many assumptions. Briefly they are that work effort is natural to mankind; that man is capable of self-control and direction;

[1] *The Human Side of Enterprise*, 1960, chapter 3.

that there is satisfaction in achievement, apart from rewards; that people can not only learn to bear responsibility but to look for it; that ingenuity and creative imagination are widely possessed characteristics; and that under modern industrial conditions the potentialities of people are being only partially utilized.

Theory Y sounds almost like a manifesto on behalf of ordinary working men and women everywhere, and in a sense it is. As McGregor says, the six assumptions carry sharply different implications for management from the three of Theory X. They are positive instead of negative; optimistic instead of pessimistic; dynamic instead of static. 'They are not framed in terms of the least common denominator of the factory hand, but in terms of a resource which has substantial potentialities.' They are also, for a great many hardened, cynical and perhaps disillusioned industrialists, hard to swallow. And yet there is abundant evidence that Theory Y is much closer to the elusive truth of the matter than Theory X. The benefits of making it come true would be considerable. To quote McGregor once more:

'Many managers would agree that the effectiveness of their organizations would be at least doubled if they could discover how to tap the unrealized potential present in their human resources.'

Returning for a moment to past examples of progressive management, we find that early this century there were businessmen who instinctively strove to make the best of their human resources. Hans Renold, the second example of scientific management in practice chosen by Urwick and Brech, set up his engineering works in 1879. From the outset Renold wanted to recruit, train and keep high grade labour. 'One great and helpful element in our organization,' he told the Manchester Association of Engineers, 'is the fact that from an early date we have taken great care with young men and have established a carefully graded apprenticeship system, offering every facility for learning, and giving liberal remunerations, which are always attractive to ambitious youths. We thus secured a good supply of young men of good character, very often the sons of our own workmen or foremen.' As well as technical training, these same young men were later shown how to take responsibility and to become managers themselves. Like Monsieur Jourdain with his prose, Hans Renold was putting Theory Y into practice without knowing it. In the official history of the company he is credited with 'a practical contribution in a number of ways to the new social idealism which was ceasing to regard the employee as a mere "hand"; both in his original business and in its successor he was consistently among the pioneers of better human relations in industry'.[1]

By 1913 the company was employing about 1,350 people in two works, with a wide range of products covering all kinds of driving chains and sprockets, a large overseas market, and an advanced subdivision of processes. The organization chart with which Hans Renold kept track of his company's structure and the allocation of duties appears in Urwick and Brech, and must be among the earliest of its kind. It subdivides the company into five departments, general services, chain and wheel manufacturing, equipment manufacturing, selling and research, and even descends into a sixth or sub-service department that includes the kitchen and the door-keeper. It is interesting, too, that the general services included an employment manager 'responsible for general discipline'.

Renold seems to have been exceptional in at least two ways. He systematically kept in touch, through a network of staff meetings, with his departments, allowing them all the scope in discussion that would call forth their ideas and criticisms. And just as systematically he paid attention to his labour force, its recruitment, training and development. He considered but never introduced the Taylor system, whereby, in the great engineer's own words, 'it is possible to double the output of the men and their machines just as they stand now . . .'. But he was acutely aware that any attempt to speed up work and output would require 'men of tact and power to lead'.[2]

On the other hand, the notion was well rooted in the minds of employers and their engineers that, far from working as quickly as possible, workers deliberately worked as slowly as possible. 'Every workman, from the time that he started to serve his apprenticeship, was deliberately taught by the men who were older than himself that it was to his best interests to "soldier", as Americans called it, or to "hang it out", as Englishmen called it, instead of going fast'.[3]

[1] Basil Tripp, *Renold Chains*, 1956, p. 20.
[2] Urwick and Brech, *op. cit.*, pp. 94 and 169.
[3] Urwick and Brech, *op. cit.*, p. 95.

In the United States, instead of relying on human goodwill, they had taken to measuring work and, by the time that Frederick Winslow Taylor was lecturing on his system to British manufacturers, motion study had been in use in their factories for over thirty years, and Gilbreth had been applying it in the building industry for four. But the First World War came before British industry had had time to do more than argue the merits of what came to be known as 'scientific management', though Hans Renold claimed to have adapted Taylor's tabulated common sense, as he described it, and applied it in his own workshops.

Not surprisingly, the question of the effect on individual freedom of the close control exercised by the Taylor system was also a point of controversy. Urwick and Brech record the discussion led by Edward Cadbury in 1913 at the Sociological Society, in which J. A Hobson, the historian of capitalism and imperialism, inveighed against a system which threatened to sacrifice human initiative and freedom to efficiency, and Hans Renold's son Charles testified to its value to industry.[1] Little or no comment is recorded on behalf of the trade unions, presumably because as yet they had no actual cause to take note of Taylorism.

The arrival of what came to be time and motion study is a landmark in the development of industrial relations in Britain. It pinpoints a stage in the emergence of the study and application of management which begins to take into account the behaviour of the people on the shop floor. But it looks at their behaviour from the point of view of the engineer and the accountant, and in no other way.

By making the individual worker more productive scientific management also made it possible for the progressive employer to compete more successfully with those who deliberately refrained from spending any money at all on welfare or who exploited their 'hands' quite ruthlessly. Asa Briggs has demonstrated that one of the forces which compelled the enlightened employers to seek legislation about working conditions and shorter hours was the very fear that if they simply put them into effect in their own factories 'the very small shop working very long hours' would be more potent,[2] and they would lose busi-

[1] Vol. II, p. 101.
[2] Flanders and Clegg, *The System of Industrial Relations in Great Britain*, 1954, p. 7.

ness. But the Factory Acts sedulously avoided doing more than protect women and young persons and make regulations about safety. The hours of work and the wages of adult males were left to the market forces to settle, on the tenuous assumption that the male adult worker and his employer were equally matched parties to the employment bargain or contract. Kahn-Freund has described this freedom to contract, even when the worker was impelled by sheer necessity to take whatever employment he was offered on any terms, as 'fictitious', but it nevertheless was influential as a principle.[1] As we shall see later, there is a natural, logical connection between this fiction of equality and the emergence of collective bargaining.

Looking at the industrial relations scene in those years immediately preceding the First World War it is not difficult to grasp the feelings of organized labour. On the shop floor their members were either attempting to wring concessions out of the employers in terms of time or money or being subjected to the benefits of scientific management coupled with paternalistic welfare schemes. These three developments emerged almost simultaneously, with time and motion study a bad third. Employers' benevolence could be discerned a century earlier in isolated cases, but developed mightily under men like Edward Cadbury and W. H. Lever with his Port Sunlight formula. Lever, talking of profit sharing, which he preferred to call 'prosperity sharing' said:

'If I were to follow the usual mode of profit sharing I would send my workmen and work girls to the cash office at the end of each year and say to them: "You are going to receive £8 each; you have earned this money: it belongs to you. Take it and make whatever use you like of your money." Instead of that I told them: "£8 is an amount which is soon spent, and it will not do you much good if you send it down your throats in the form of bottles of whisky, bags of sweets, or fat geese for Christmas. On the other hand, if you leave this money with me, I shall use it to provide for you everything which makes life pleasant—viz. nice houses, comfortable homes, and healthy recreation. Besides, I am disposed to allow profit sharing under no other form."[2]

In one paragraph the first Lord Leverhulme managed to

---

[1] Flanders and Clegg, *op. cit.*, pp. 45–6.
[2] Charles Wilson, *The History of Unilever*, 1954, Vol. I, pp. 146–7.

sum up all the prejudices of the employing class. First, he assumed that he was entitled to withhold weekly payment from 'his people' and make some arbitrary adjustment to their income annually. The workpeople themselves probably accepted this tamely enough, but union leaders would not have. Many of them would have argued that the 'profits' that were being shared had largely arisen from previous underpayment of labour. This particular bone of contention is still being gnawed. Secondly, he assumed that even if he had handed over to his workers this trivial sum, it would soon be squandered on luxurious food and drink, and that he, in his greater wisdom, could spend it better on their behalf. Finally, whatever the arguments or whether they are accepted or not, he will do what he pleases. Such public statements (this one was apparently a newspaper interview) would hardly go unnoticed by the new and militant mass unions, and the reaction of the intelligent unionist to this blend of benevolence and tyranny may be imagined. W. H. Lever's feelings about trade unions were not untypical of his class and period. He accepted them with reluctance and fought them when he had to, sometimes using his 'co-partnership' scheme as a weapon. The unions had shown themselves opposed to profit-sharing in any form. They would not therefore be surprised to find that, during a strike, loyal 'co-partners' who went on working were rewarded by the management. Charles Wilson quotes Lever on strikes: 'neglect of duty . . . wilful misconduct . . . disloyalty to employers . . . or a breach of the undertaking'. He comments, 'one is tempted to ask whether the author of co-partnership, sincere as his motives were, fully realised the delicacy and difficulty of the problems of industrial relations, involving as they did human rights and aspirations as well as material benefits'.[1]

No doubt Lever, like most of his contemporaries, regarded his business as his own (he kept complete control of all the ordinary share capital all his life) and hotly resented any attempt by interlopers, whether managers or workers, to resist his policy or decision making. As Wilson says, 'Co-partnership was only possible in this business because the voting power of the Ordinary shares lay with one man. . . . Labour costs were low in the soap industry. The co-partnership scheme had the virtues and vices implied in one description of it: "The scheme amounted

[1] *Op. cit.*, Vol. I, pp. 156.

to an annual gift out of his own pocket as sole Ordinary share-holder".'

Lever himself had once said in a speech that the British working man had a profound distrust and dislike of paternalism, which suggests that he was blind to the nature of the clash of opinion between him and his kind and the leaders of the various labour movements. While the leaders of opinion on the Left were talking in terms of industrial democracy (having seen the spread of political democracy over the previous seventy years), businessmen like the late Viscount Leverhulme were setting up so-called partnerships in which the working classes in their employment took no effective part at all.

The official historian of Unilever does his best to plead the case for this sort of enlightened despotism. 'It was, we can now see, unreasonable to expect that all the problems of industrial relations could be solved by one man with two schemes. Inevitably their success was limited. But the real value of these schemes did not lie in the immediate success or failure which they achieved but in the new attitude and heightened effort which they represented. In an industrial era still suffering from the necessarily hasty improvization of earlier decades, Lever's model factory and village, his treatment of his workers—standard wages, a pension scheme, and a score of welfare schemes—were an attempt to embody enlightenment in a system. Despotic the management might be, but it pressed most hardly on the upper layers of society. The directors suffered the slings and arrows; the workers enjoyed the benevolence'.

A trade unionist might want to ask at that point how much the directors were paid for their sufferings, and perhaps question the use of the word 'enjoy', except in the special sense of experience. For it is here that the trade union member who thinks about his situation at all deeply parts company with the 'do-gooders'. The working man, he would almost certainly argue, wants a just reward for his labours. There have been many arguments about the ways and means in which the calculations about work and pay should be done, and what the answers might be. But on the whole, apart from preferring pleasant working conditions to bad, the worker likes his reward in cash. Fringe benefits tend to be taken for granted today, and they are not resented in the way in which the livelier spirits would have resented the Big Brotherly atmosphere of Port Sunlight. But the suspicion lingers on that 'they', the management and the proprietors, are inclined to hold back some of the fruits of labour. The tangle of time and piece rate schemes all over Britain testifies to the amount of effort that has gone over the years into solving this key problem. The Fawley Agreement at Esso Petroleum, which was heralded as the dawn of an era in which restrictive practices would successively be bargained away, is only one of many attempts at satisfying the demands of labour. Evidently Theory Y is not enough on its own.

CHAPTER III

PERSONNEL MANAGEMENT AND SOCIAL SCIENCE

THROUGHOUT British industry the engineer (whom we would now refer to as technologist) and the accountant are still the key figures in most enterprises. Their specializations emerged and were codified and institutionalized quite early in the course of the development of industry. The engineers, both civil and mechanical, were 'professionalized' by the middle of the nineteenth century. The accountants were somewhat later, and did not begin to work in industry in any numbers until after the passing of the Companies Act in 1862.[1] Their importance in the smallest firm is undeniable and the leadership of successful businesses tends more and more to fall into their hands.

Alongside the growth and establishment of these two, the personnel or labour manager appears as a rather new specialist. Most companies preferred to leave the recruitment, training and control of labour in the hands of general management or of the proprietors, on the lines of Boulton and Watt. The exceptional company, perhaps the more farsighted or better organized, like Hans Renold's, sometimes fastened the responsibility on one member of the Board or the senior management. At Siemens in Woolwich, a subsidiary of the German parent, Siemens und Halske, the tough paternalism developed by Werner von Siemens prevailed.

Men were taken on and laid off as the business of cable making fluctuated with general commercial conditions. 'Officially, the firm re-employed the old hands who had been laid off; in practice the choice was made from the large crowd which each morning waited at the gates.' The official history of Siemens records also that 'The foremen were as arbitrary as they were powerful; they were commonly believed to hire men who had bought them beer'.[2] But alongside 'the discipline and the

[1] Carr-Saunders and Wilson, *The Professions*, 1933, pp. 161 *et seq.* and 210 *et seq.*
[2] J. D. Scott, *Siemens Brothers, 1858–1958*, 1958, p. 248.

laissez-faire harshness, however, was a sense of comradeship and kindness. A boy who looked peaky was sent off by Alexander Siemens for a spell at his house in the country where there was a dormitory above the stables for this purpose.' But 'the standards of welfare were of course the standards of the day, and by our standards they were not high. In the early days at Woolwich, "there was no provision made whatever for the workers to warm their food or make a cup of tea during the winter months. It was a pitiful sight to see men and boys walking about during the meal hours eating their cold food. . . ." ' Later warming troughs and a frying pan were provided.

The history claims, nevertheless, that 'the paternal policy of labour relations which Siemens and Halske had pioneered both in Germany and England was markedly successful. All through the long period from 1858 until the end of the First World War, a period running from the London builders' lock-out of 1859-60, through the great dock strike of 1889 and through the bitter struggles of 1911-12, Siemens Brothers were little troubled by strikes and stoppages. Only in 1898 was there a stoppage over a demand for a forty-eight hour week. . . .' This was settled in a manner unrevealed in Alexander Siemens personal records, except that the demand was withdrawn and 'the workshop rules of the employers were accepted'.

It is possible to surmise, however, that that crowd waiting at the factory gates every morning had more than a little to do with the ultimate obedience of the Siemens workers. Unemployment became, in the 1900s, a problem of important proportions for the nation as a whole, and it was far from being understood, although there were many and varied theories as to its cause. When the part solution of setting up Employment Exchanges, as a means of creating a better market for labour, was first mooted the trade unions reacted adversely, suspecting that this was yet another employers' ruse to supply blacklegs with which to break strikes or to supply cheap labour as a way of undercutting union rates.[1] This somewhat recalcitrant reaction to a benevolent move on the part of Government was clearly brought about by long years of mutual mistrust between employers and employed, now crystallized into militant mass unionism on the workers' part. The strength of the new unions which had been founded in the 1880s and onwards tended to

[1] Phelps Brown, *op. cit.*, p. 306.

support an uncompromising mood on the part of their members. After the First World War Charles Renold (now Sir Charles), writing in *British Labour* in 1920, recorded his opinion that 'the state of tension in industry is greater than ever, and the need for finding some appeasement more urgent'. By this time the employers were organized too, with the Federation of British Industries and the National Confederation of Employers' Organizations confronting the eight million and more trade union members. The bigger and stronger both sides became, it was thought by some observers, the less chance there could be of amity. Not unnaturally this mood communicated itself to individuals and to working groups.

Alongside this growing toughness of attitude on both parts there developed a certain impersonality in the workplace itself. The contrast between the close-knit friendliness and casual disorder of the individual's working-class life and the highly disciplined, aloof atmosphere of the factory is well described in the first two pages of a standard work on personnel management, Northcott's *Personnel Management* (1945), which has been circulating in industry for over twenty years. He sketches the scene in a factory at the start of the working day when the workers arrive as idiosyncratic individuals, some early, some late, most of them on time to punch the clock, singly or in groups, by all means of transport according to choice and means. But by the time they have changed their clothes and reported to their work stations they have become, willy nilly, parts of a planned operation in which their small contribution has long ago been decided by some unknown master mind.

With the growing size of the workplace under the compulsion of mass production and flow process methods and with the coming of salaried managements working for boards of directors controlled by, perhaps thousands of faceless shareholders (a constitution only vaguely understood by the average working man and woman) a measure of impersonality and remote control became unavoidable. Add to these factors the prevalent belief among employers with a background of engineering that all a factory need be was a shell in which to house machines that cost a lot of money and the state of mind of the human beings employed therein may be imagined. The use of colour and designed lighting in the workplace, well-sited lavatories, proper heating and ventilation and all the amenities now to be found in modern production units is a phenomenon of the 1950s and 1960s, and even now is not widespread, simply because most of British industry is half a century or more old.

The importance of working conditions has been argued about for years. Industrial psychologists like Dr J. A. C. Brown point to happy working groups singing and laughing in the offal sorting-room of a slaughterhouse 'below ground level, dimly lit by artificial light, cold and damp—a perfect epitome of how a workroom ought not to be. Its floors were covered with blood, water and the contents of animal's intestines which smelt collectively extremely unpleasant to the casual visitor.' The girls, records Dr Brown, evidently an eye-witness, refused to be moved to better quarters, while elsewhere in the factory in well-lit, well-heated pleasant surroundings 'hundreds of other girls worked and grumbled over their jobs'.[1]

Dr Brown adds, 'There was nothing special about the six girls in the small room' and contends that twenty years before there had been another six and that individuals had come and gone 'but morale had never been other than good'. He is attempting to separate morale from working conditions in arguing thus, and we know that people can rise superior to their conditions of considerable discomfort and even misery, especially in time of war or obvious emergency. But laughter and singing can also be the symptoms of defiance and deep-seated resentment, while hearsay reports of twenty-year-old morale need not be taken at their face value. Yet what Brown is arguing is simply that carefully designed amenities and good working conditions are not enough in themselves to raise the spirits or morale (the preferred word in this context) of workpeople, nor is it easy to prove that a particular 'improvement' has a positive effect on morale and therefore upon productivity.

The first clue to the nature of this problem was offered by the American F. J. Roethlisberger, in his book *Management and Morale* which was based on the findings of the celebrated Hawthorne Investigations at the Western Electric Company. This American company had set out to experiment with the lighting in its workrooms to discover at what intensity work could be done most efficiently. Two groups of workers were involved. One worked in unchanging conditions as the control group; the other was the 'guinea-pig' group whose lighting was

[1] *The Social Psychology of Industry*, pp. 193–4.

changed from very bright to the equivalent of full moonlight. Sometimes the second group was told that the illumination in its room had been changed when it had not. But whatever the investigators did, or merely said that they did, the output of both groups went up. This happened between 1924 and 1926, but thirty years later books and articles continued to make Hawthorne their centre.

Urwick and Brech devoted the third volume of *The Making of Scientific Management* to Hawthorne, and picked up a point from Roethlisberger when they entitled their ninth chapter 'A New Conception of Personnel Management'. Roethlisberger himself had argued that the systems of personnel management then in vogue in American industry seemed to be 'adequate in general but inadequate in particular' because they tried to address the problem in terms of general psychological principles and not of individual human beings. 'They tend to be concerned with somebody and anybody, but with nobody in particular'. In short, the labour or personnel management that industry had been gradually introducing under the pressures touched upon above was as impersonal as the factory and its machines.

Roethlisberger pointed to something else that was not much help in grappling with the problems of shop-floor relations and morale. First, the human problems tended to be separated from and studied in isolation from the technical, when it might be more fruitful to look at them jointly. Secondly, the personnel management function was apt to be regarded as an expensive necessity forced upon the firm by the unpredictability and recalcitrance of the workers. In addition, personnel policies were settled beforehand by the company's administrators, leaving the personnel department to work within its constraints and, indeed, to try to solve problems that the policy itself had created.

Personnel or labour management in its earliest form appears to have been mainly a matter of welfare amenities intended to alleviate uncomfortable and even harsh working conditions with a view to buying a measure of shop-floor goodwill. The trade unions were not much impressed with this form of charity in industry, and welfare consequently became almost a derisory expression.

The First World War compelled British factory owners to make much more rapid and systematic progress in the management of people. With plenty of money available for the production of war material of all kinds, there was a stimulus to

C

modernize plant and machines, to standardize product ranges and to conform to specific requirements in factories working on Government contracts that there should, for example, be a full-time welfare worker on the premises. Sometimes these so-called welfare workers had no training at all and reflected the casual attitude of the employers that here was an extension of the favours that they were being made to grant. Not surprisingly the workers' response was unsympathetic.[1] There was nothing automatic about the employers' response to the cajoling of officials like the Director of the Welfare Department of the Ministry of Munitions, Seebohm Rowntree. When this former labour director of an enlightened family chocolate firm asked a particular employer to raise the standards of welfare in his works the man answered that he was not interested in Mr Rowntree's hobby. He had a hobby of his own, collecting old china, and he did not expect Rowntree to be interested in that.[2]

This gulf between the thinking of the enlightened employer and what might be called the Theory X school remained (and still does here and there) long after the practice of personnel management and industrial welfare had been confirmed by the establishment of associations to which the practitioners could belong and through which they could support one another and propagate their calling. The war had inspired the Ministry of Munitions to set up a Health and Welfare Department (particularly in the interests of women and young people) and an Industrial Fatigue Research Board. Out of these emerged the Industrial Welfare Society (which has now dropped the word welfare from its name) and University College, London, established an Industrial Psychology Group. The National Institute of Industrial Psychology was founded in 1920. The personnel managers, significantly known in the early days as industrial welfare workers, had been organized on a small scale before the war, became a professional association during the war and took their present title as the Institute of Personnel Management in 1931. This happening could be seen as a step forward from the charitable image of industrial welfare work towards a more systematic, quasi-scientific handling of works relations. Just how far that is true would be difficult to say. The study and practice of industrial psychology, however, seems to

---

[1] Cf. Briggs in Flanders and Clegg, *op. cit.*, p. 37.
[2] Asa Briggs, *Seebohm Rowntree*, 1961, p. 86 n.

play a minor part in the training of personnel managers in modern industry, the emphasis being, if one is to judge from the books they study and from the syllabus of the I.P.M.'s approved course, rather more on administration in its various forms, law, economics, statistics, wages systems, and related matters of a routine nature. This is not the fault of the personnel managers themselves but rather may be blamed on the traditionalist attitudes of Britain's educational and research institutions, especially the universities. As Miss Nancy Seear has said, 'The tradition of British universities was not favourable to the development of the human sciences, which until World War II did not begin to compete with the older academic disciplines in status, in financial resources, *or in the career opportunities available to their students.* Psychology departments were established in most universities during the interwar period, but were mainly small in scale; while sociology, as understood today, was not studied at all in the majority of British universities'.[1]

Accustomed as we are in modern industrial Britain to saying and thinking that this is the age of technology, or some such catchphrase, we tend to forget how backward we are in the human sciences, with the various schools of psychologists still fighting desultory campaigns against one another and with barely a score of trained industrial sociologists at work in industry. By trained, of course, one means on the whole that those graduate sociologists who have chosen industry as their area of inquiry have also worked alongside an experienced colleague on an industrial investigation. The first degree of one of Britain's leading industrial sociologists, taken before there were degrees in sociology, is in mediaeval history.

In her chapter in *Society*, Miss Seear recounts briefly the patchy history of the behavioural sciences in British industry She points out, significantly, that there are tremendous gaps in knowledge, that industrial behaviour is one of them. Although individual and group psychology have received a growing amount of attention in the past twenty years, mainly stimulated by wartime conditions and the need to understand and handle (solve would be too sweeping a word) difficult human situations, 'broader problems of the relations of industry to the community and of the relations between the unions and employers and between unions and unions have been studied only

---

[1] 'Industrial Research in Britain,' in *Society*, 1962, p. 171. Our italics.

descriptively or by statistical analysis'. One might add that this has never inhibited employers, trade union leaders, politicians and other commentators from making sweeping and often harmful generalizations about labour relations.

In his book *The British Worker*, which is not what might be called an academic monograph, supported by statistics or profound research, but a thoughtful commentary mainly derived from interviews, Ferdinand Zweig has a chapter headed 'The Neglected Human Side in Industry'.[1] Here he has some quotations that have a familiar ring and would certainly bring an impatient frown to some middle-class brows. 'My employer never looks at me, he just sees the £.s.d. I represent. For him I am manpower, not a man.' 'Men are treated here as part of the machinery...but the funny part of it is that they are not studied as the machines are, and kept in good running order.' 'The capitalists say to the worker: "I am going to use you to get rich".'

Even if these statements are not accurate, it is important to ask why they should be made at all. Zweig attributes it largely to what he calls excessive commercialism, the 'labour market' approach to the employment of people, leading to the inevitable comment from a working man that the relationship between boss and worker was nothing more than the buying and selling of labour.

One employer argued that this was unavoidable because 'business isn't charity or a club . . . it's fatal to be sentimental in your work. You are being unfair to others who rely on your employment. Business is a hard struggle to make a living for others and yourself against very sharp competition'. Has anyone ever asked (they have certainly not answered) the question why it is always the workpeople and sometimes higher grade employees who are the object of sociological and psychological inquiry and rarely the entrepreneurs and managers? One answer is in the minds of all human scientists in industry. It is the managerial and directing group that has the power to permit or refuse investigations in industry, and so far there are not enough company directors broadminded and tolerant enough to allow themselves to be included. They would probably argue that it is for them that the work of the social scientists is being done.

[1] Published in 1952: p. 115 *et seq.*

CHAPTER IV

TRADE UNIONS AND COLLECTIVE BARGAINING

THE key to the understanding of industrial relations in Britain or anywhere lies in grasping the essential character of the wages bargain struck between employer and employed, in various working situations at various times. No matter what the state of trade or what the relative strengths of the two bargainers, Professor Phelps Brown's terse summing up holds largely true, that the wage earner's need of a job is more immediate than the employers need of him and, therefore, whenever there are more vacancies than jobs he is likely to get the worst of the wage-bargain.[1]

There have been occasions, and today they are more numerous than ever, when the wage earner's bargaining position is strong, sometimes by luck, sometimes by arrangement (as when a union has calculatedly brought about a shortage of skilled labour in its own trade). And when, on such occasions, there is a suggestion of labour 'getting its own back' it may be attributed to all those past occasions when 'its own' was taken away, or appeared to be. Deeply ingrained in the thinking of trade unions and labour organizations with their roots in the nineteenth century is the basic tenet that a man has a right to work. Whatever else may be said, joblessness is not a condition that most men willingly seek. If this is taken to be a truism, well and good. If not, the starting point of all reasoning about labour relations is wrong because, like a piece of bad navigation, it will go increasingly wrong and diverge, eventually widely, from a true and successful course.

Men want to work. If they are really fortunate, they also like to work. There are many things they have done and will do to stay in employment, from machine breaking to the present

[1] E. H. Phelps Brown, *The Growth of British Industrial Relations*, 1959, p. xvi.

forms of 'neo-Luddism'. Neither of these phenomena is desirable and both can be avoided, along with all (or nearly all) restrictive practices, as they have come to be known. But a sympathy, in the precise meaning of the word, a fellow feeling, has to be conjured up before any constructive exchange of ideas can take place, especially if any permanent progress is to be made.

For these reasons alone it is important for employers and managers, if they are not the same person, to be aware of the way in which the organizations of labour have evolved, and how they and their members have changed with the times. For if some trade unions have not rewritten their rule books in conformity with the ideas of the mid-twentieth century, as contrasted with those of the mid-nineteenth, many of their practices have kept pace. It is no uncommon thing to find a 'modern' union with a streamlined research department on the one hand and a line of official thinking on the other that would have sounded familiar to a Victorian proprietor.

Trade unions began, as far as can be established with any certainty, in the craft industries, no doubt because among them there were above average intelligences among the tradesmen, and also because of the existing familiarity with trade organizations through knowledge of the craft guild system and the yeoman or journeyman guilds. In their early years they functioned mainly as friendly societies and only to a limited extent as bargaining organizations.

But from the outset there is little doubt that one of their prime motives was to increase the security of their members, not so much against the whims and caprices of their masters, but rather against the unpredictable hazards of life: injury and sickness, loss of work, death and bereavement. There was also a strong social element in the craft unions' meetings, which was one reason that they took place in public houses, as many of them still do. Another of course, was that there was seldom anywhere else for a number of men to meet under cover.

All this is by way of arguing that in their early years the combinations of trades, as they were called, were not collective bargaining organizations primarily, but mutual aid societies of journeymen or day labourers, many of whom found it impossible ever to become master craftsmen in their trades after the guild system was decayed to the point where the existing masters and liverymen had closed their ranks. There is a nice irony in the resemblance between the seventeenth- and eighteenth-century guilds, with their refusal to pursue the old ways and allow the time-served journeyman to aspire to master's status, thus adding to competition in the trade, and the nineteenth- and twentieth-century trade union with its limitation on the number of apprentices that may be employed in a particular shop.

The weakness of the labour bargain on the worker's side was recognized and tacitly admitted in the days of Elizabeth I, whose Statute of Artificers, with its wage-fixing arrangements, was repealed in 1813. It and the various Acts surrounding it, as well as the machinery for assessing 'fair wages' (it was supposed to be done at quarter sessions by a panel of Justices of the Peace), had long fallen into disuse. Indeed, the Home Secretary in 1813, Lord Sidmouth, had said in the Parliamentary debate that the very existence of this legislation had been forgotten by the legal authorities themselves. Meanwhile, conditions among the labourers and their families, especially in the countryside where the majority were employed, had declined to the point where those very J.P.s who had failed to uphold the Elizabethan law in all its antique justice, had devised a kind of dole whereby deserving cases in certain counties only (in fact, where the ratepayers would put up with the expense) were to receive a weekly bread allowance. This was the Speenhamland system, originating in Berkshire.

It did not accord with the Adam Smith conception of *laisser-faire*, of course. In Smith's view the day labourers should have been allowed to combine and bargain from strength with their employers. While not specifically outlawed until the wartime enactments of 1799 and 1800, trade unions were still liable to be prosecuted as unlawful conspiracies, but to bring suit against a combination that might simply dissolve, as so many did without undue pressure, before the sessions met, was cumbersome and expensive. Hence the widespread support for the so-called Combination Laws, which made illegal even the social gatherings themselves, let alone the collections of money that had hitherto been made for the benefit of widows and orphans, unfortunate fellow members and other victims of circumstance.

There was, in fact, as wide a rift between the thinking of masters and men in the Napoleonic era on the subject of trade unions as there is now between management and labour on the matter of unofficial strikes. To the craftsmen of the late eighteenth and early nineteenth century to band together for mutual aid and protection was nothing more than natural. To their employers, already apprehensive on account of the machine breaking that they had witnessed among the framework knitters and shearmen (cloth finishers) as well as the horror stories of revolution and Jacobinism that were crossing the Channel, this was dangerous insubordination and conspiracy, to be put down with all the firmness that the law could command.

It was also believed that the formation of unions would drive up the general level of wages, which for a short time it did, after the repeal of the Combination Acts in 1824, the reaction of some workers to the emancipating legislation skilfully secured by Francis Place and Joseph Hume being to band together and demand, as the Sheffield cutlers did, double wages for a three-day week. But that was the age of the classical economists, who believed in the wisdom of allowing the market freely to settle prices and wages. While detailed experience did not support this *laisser-faire* philosophy at all points, eventually the unions came to see that there was something in the view that demand and supply could interact to affect the price of labour.

Accordingly unionism went through a phase when it learnt to restrict supply by means of controlling entry to a trade, by sending men out of a district where business in a trade was slack, and even by subsidizing emigration from the country altogether. This was hardly collective bargaining. It was more an attempt to create favourable conditions in the labour market by more subtle, long-term action. Naturally, it did not appeal to the militant elements in the trade union movement, and such tactics did nothing to improve the lot of the unskilled worker whose market for labour was impossible to manipulate in this manner.

It was the use of growing numbers of semi-skilled and unskilled workers in the new industries like transport and gas and the emergence of large unorganized labour forces on the docks and in the General Post Office that created the conditions in the 1880s in which it was possible to establish successful general and industrial unions. It had been attempted before, with comparatively little success. Under the circumstances of the late nineteenth century, with better communications and with more than half a century of union experience to draw upon, it seems inevitable that mass unionism should have flourished. The strength of such unions when it came to collective bargaining was hardly to be doubted. The Gas, Light and Coke Company and the South Metropolitan Gas Company capitulated swiftly enough in the summer of 1889 when faced with Will Thorne's National Union of Gasworkers and General Labourers, demanding an eight-hour day without loss of pay. But the Great Dock Strike was a hard-fought battle, by contrast, for a less spectacular gain.

This militant, mass union organization has come to be called the New Unionism, as opposed to the more sedate and thoughtful New Model Unions of the mid-nineteenth century. It called into existence an equally militant counter-attack on the part of employers who, hitherto, had not been particularly well organized, but saw the value of federating in the face of the growing confederations of labour. This was the formative period of collective bargaining. Until the 1890s only in the cotton industry was there anything resembling a national agreement. By the outbreak of the First World War national agreements had been signed in the iron and steel industry, shipbuilding, building, engineering and a number of other industries. The Royal Commission on Labour, reporting in 1894, recorded its acceptance of the emergence of a highly organized bargaining system between employers and labour and expressed approval of the existence of regular negotiating machinery. 'We hope and believe' said their final report, 'that the present rapid extension of voluntary boards will continue.' In addition to this formalization of collective bargaining, the Government of the day took an increasing interest in industrial relations, to the extent that it was remarked that Presidents of the Board of Trade like Churchill and Lloyd George were on the verge of exceeding the duties expected of them.[1]

At the same time, the tensions between employers and unions and the strikes stemming from them, demonstrated that the simple existence of collective bargaining machinery was not in itself a solution. The economic pressures to which employing firms were subject, and particularly the cyclical movements of trade, enforced wage reductions which the unions refused to countenance. Even if the union leaders, with more knowledge

---

[1] Clegg, Fox and Thompson, *A History of British Trade Unions since 1889*, Vol. I, p. 466 *et seq.*

than their members and more sophistication, tried to understand the financial predicaments of the employers who faced them across the negotiating table, the rank and file was inclined to suspect that they were 'out of touch'. In fact, it was the membership that was out of touch, disinclined as it was to face unwelcome truths. Whatever the basic cause, one may date from these years an uneasiness among trade union members regarding the efficacy of collective bargaining. More than half a century ago the first cracks appeared in trade union solidarity between the leadership at national level and the local, militant rank and file.

The unwelcome truth was that, in the first ten years of this century, there was no rise in real wages, increases in money incomes failing on the whole to keep pace with price increases. There is an interesting parallel between those years and our own in that economic historians estimate that between 1900 and 1910 there was a fall in home investment in favour of foreign, a large rise in what we would now call defence spending by the Government, a decline in Britain's industrial supremacy in the world (partly because the rate of technological innovation had slowed down, partly because of the rise of Germany and the United States) and no discernible increase in industrial output or productivity per worker. Commentators at the time were inclined to put the blame for the consequences of all these on union restrictive practices. Trade unionists themselves felt disappointed with the material results of their new and powerful movement, and were all for blaming their leadership. The main culprit was the unfavourable terms of trade that set in after 1900, with exports fetching less and imports costing more. But to both employers and employed it was simpler to blame each other.

The union leadership itself seemed to find the machinery of collective bargaining congenial and workable, but it brought with it both a strong tendency to establish national rather than local organization and the need to appoint many more full-time officials. Clegg, Fox and Thompson suggest that at this time the number of full-time union officers was growing faster than the membership that they served. They also point out that trade unions had achieved acceptance by this time, not on philosophical grounds, the right to freedom of association and similar liberal tenets, but because they were in a position to work alongside the employers in maintaining industrial order. It was at this juncture, of course, that the network of official conciliation boards, joint committees and arbitration procedures began more and more to formalize employer-union relationships, and to raise the level of negotiation and bargaining well above the shop floor and the local branch.

Without stretching the parallel beyond endurance, it is worth noting that the years when large-scale unionism and its bargaining apparatus were in process of formation were also the years when the foundations of what we now call the Welfare State were laid. The Budget of 1908 supported Lloyd George's Old Age Pensions Act by stepping up income tax; Beveridge's national system of Labour Exchanges was initiated in 1909 in an attempt to establish some kind of rational market for labour; and the National Insurance Act of 1911 made the first essay in unemployment insurance and convenanted health benefits. In 1907 the Government had first begun to distinguish in taxation between earned and unearned incomes.

These were the foundations of the Welfare State framework in which trade unions were to find themselves working under the post-1945 Labour Governments. Contrary to common belief, the Welfare State was not a 'socialist' invention, any more than had been the setting up and widening of industry-wide bargaining. All three parties to the tacit agreement to pursue both the enlargement of national welfare and the improvement of the wage bargaining machinery stood to gain, in theory at least. Clearly the workers hoped for material gains, the Government for industrial peace (to use the phrase current before the First World War) and the employers for fewer strikes and other interruptions in production.

But it was the unions that set the pace, even to the extent of compelling the Government first to assist companies and industries to establish an employers' side of the negotiating body where there was none, and later to set up boards and councils to adjust bargains between both sides in unorganized (that is, un-unionized) industries. The employers quickly saw another advantage in wide collective agreements. It enabled them to pay the 'going rate' in their industry, because all their competitors would come under the same negotiated scales. Conversely, some trade unionists saw a too-efficient employers' side as a kind of wage-restricting cartel.

Either way, the expansion of wage fixing beyond local branches and one firm, or a handful of firms meant that men in the same industry all across the country had an opportunity to learn, for the first time, how their wages compared with their fellows some hundreds of miles away, in a part of the country they had never seen and knew nothing about, but which might unexpectedly be revealed as prosperous by contrast with their own. This could, and sometimes did, force up wages in areas of low employment, with the attendant risk of further unemployment if and when the employers tried to reduce costs by installing machinery.

Both unions and employers therefore had ambivalent opinions of collective bargaining and, as far as the company itself was concerned, it put a strain on it as a social institution that brought into being (admittedly at first under the compulsion of wartime conditions) the part-time dues collecting union officer, the shop steward, whose role was far from clear or acceptable to employers and managers, and created a need for some additional channel of communication between management and labour. It was the Whitley Committee that first proposed the ill-starred joint consultation committees that were supposed to bridge the gap in the firm made by the external formalities of bargaining. But many managers found such committees an unwarrantable interference with their authority, while the trade union officers outside the firm could not fail to see the works council as a short-circuiting of their authority over their members. (The joint consultation phase of labour relations is examined in detail in Chapter X, and the emergence of the shop steward in the chapter after this.)

The legislative background of collective bargaining is set out in the *Industrial Relations Handbook*, published by the Ministry of Labour, and periodically revised. But even today the main enactments supporting the official bargaining structure remain the Conciliation Act of 1896 and the Industrial Courts Act of 1919. It was a Royal Commission on Trades Disputes and Trade Combinations in 1891 that initiated the Act which underlies the Ministry of Labour's conciliation service. It was the Whitley Committee Report of 1918 that gave rise to the arbitration procedure to which the two parties to an industrial dispute may voluntarily refer their differences. Under this Act the Minister of Labour is empowered to set up a court of inquiry into an industrial dispute.

J. H. Whitley was the Deputy Speaker of the House of Commons to whom was entrusted the chairmanship of a Committee on the Relations between Employers and Employed during the troubled war years when the ordinary machinery of collective bargaining was largely in abeyance under the Munitions of War Act, and the Shop Stewards Movement (especially strong on the Clyde) had captured a militant and unofficial following as a consequence. It was the evident friction between employers and labour, in spite of the fact that the wartime arbitration machinery was being used widely by the trade unions and that its findings were binding on both sides, that compelled the Government of the day to ask Whitley's Committee to find a way of improving the 'industrial conditions affecting the relations between employers and workmen . . .'.

The five reports of the Committee, one of which is referred to above (the fourth), suggested the formation of joint industrial councils in the better organized industries and of works committees within companies, that the statutory regulation of wages in less well organized industries should be extended, that there should be a permanent court of arbitration, and that the Ministry of Labour should have power to order inquiries. Within this framework, which still basically surrounds the collective bargaining system in Britain, the two sides of industry should be able to continue making voluntary settlements, argued the Committee, always provided that both were adequately organized.

As part of the bargaining apparatus Joint Industrial Councils were encouraged and, although some were dissolved between the wars, many were created and there are still some hundreds in being, covering a wide range of industry. They are not uniform in constitution or function, and not all of them bear the name of J.I.C., but many of them operate according to the Ministry's 'model constitution' which appears as an appendix to the *Industrial Relations Handbook*. The principle reiterated therein is that such Councils should work according to the needs of a particular industry and not in any hard-and-fast way laid down by authority. Wartime conditions apart, it is an interesting speculation as to why employers and labour failed to establish satisfactory joint negotiating machinery themselves in the first place, and how long they would have taken to do it (for eventually they would have had to do something on these lines) left to themselves.

One basic reason is not far to seek. Private enterprise is not merely a convenient expression for describing a type of commercial initiative that existed and flourished long before advanced communities had begun to develop other more public forms of business undertaking. Private enterprise has always been to a large extent private, that is proprietorial. Even when family firms grew too big to depend entirely on home-grown managerial talent, they remained private in the sense that they resented outside interference with their business, whether it was in the form of the Factory Acts with their attempts at humane regulation of working hours for children and women, whether it was a community striving to protect its clean rivers or its atmosphere from the effluents and effluvia of factory production, or whether it was a trade union 'organizing' its labour.

The last, in fact, was probably most deeply resented, if only because originally it not only had no official support, but was positively against the public interest according to the prevalent law. Employers were reluctant to acknowledge the existence or necessity of trade unions, so it is hardly surprising that at no stage would they go half-way to meet them as far as negotiating machinery was concerned. We have to remember that the 'bargain', as the employer saw it from the outset, was his to make—from strength, as the boss. This viewpoint is not dead even today. Therefore the employers were seldom on the initiative, while the unions, after more than a century of development in the face of continuous adverse pressures, were more than ready both to amalgamate and federate to strengthen their position, and to welcome positive measures by the Government that would put them regularly in touch with the employers. It was only when the massive strength of the big unions, after several amalgamations of the kind that produced the National Union of Railwaymen and the Transport and General Workers' Union, was borne in upon the consciousness of the employers and their managers that they realized that it was more than time that they, too, set up a system.

Ironically, as Professor B. C. Roberts points out in his *Trade Unions in a Free Society*,[1] the trend towards industry-wide bargaining leads eventually to a national wages policy, with no bargaining at all, thus depriving the unions of their main justification for existence. Even though they pay lip service to

[1] 2nd ed., 1962, p. 18.

the notion of a State-controlled economy, with the minimum of private business undertakings, unionists would hardly want to see a centralized system established that would reduce their function in society to almost nothing but organizers of a kind of trade or industrial friendly society. But that is the logic of it.

CHAPTER V

THE BRITISH SYSTEM OF INDUSTRIAL RELATIONS

A PARALLEL could be drawn between the national system of industrial relations and the organization structure of the individual firm. Just as an 'informal organization' develops inside a company, regardless of the organization chart's picture of who reports to whom, so in British industrial relations unofficial developments take place that sometimes cut across and even interfere with the official negotiating machinery. This machinery is now very complicated, as a study of the *Industrial Relations Handbook* quickly reveals.

At the hub of the system stands the Ministry of Labour, which in the last resort bears the responsibility for preserving what used to be called industrial peace, and for restoring it when the factions in a dispute have tried out all the procedures available without coming to a settlement. The Handbook phrases it in official language. 'Statutory provision has therefore been made for assistance to be available for preventing and settling differences in these circumstances.' Since 1918 the Ministry has had an Industrial Relations Department, with regional offices, the duties of which are to keep the voluntary machinery in good running order, to try and prevent industrial disputes and to help to settle them when they occur, to offer advice on personnel management and joint consultation (there is a Personnel Management Advisory Service to which employers may have recourse), and to administer the wages council policy and apparatus. The three ways in which the Ministry is empowered to go about its business are simply conciliation, arbitration when conciliation has not succeeded, and the last resort of formal inquiry or investigation, all of which dovetail into each other. The Conciliation Act of 1896 and the Industrial Courts Act of 1919 are still the main sources of legislative authority for such proceedings, as we saw in the last chapter. It is the first of these that prescribes the procedure through which the Minister may either bring the dissentient parties together for further talks under an independent chairman, or appoint a conciliation board, or an individual conciliator. Under the second statute the Minister may take any steps he sees fit to bring about a settlement of a dispute reported to him by either party. Often this means reference to the Industrial Court, which is a tribunal not a court of law, independent of Government or Civil Service. Its decisions are unenforceable, but once they are accepted its findings become part of the contract of employment between two parties.

The Court, which is also an advisory body for the Minister, is one of three forms of arbitration, the other two being a board of arbitration, appointed for the duration of the dispute, and individual arbitrators. There is no compulsion on either party to take part in arbitration (and there have been some awkward situations as a result), the awards are not binding, and before any of this can happen it is necessary to have worked right through the compulsory procedure of the industry concerned. It is little wonder that impatience is sometimes expressed with a routine that may suit the mood and temperament of civil servants accustomed to committee work, but appears both long drawn out and obscure to the overburdened manager or dissatisfied factory worker. A wise management does not go to arbitration without the agreement of the unions to accept the findings.

When no settlement of a dispute seems to be possible (a dispute is officially defined as 'any dispute or difference between employers and workmen, or between workmen and workmen connected with the employment or non-employment, or the terms of employment or with the conditions of labour of any person') the Minister may resort to the appointment of a committee of investigation, if it is a small affair, or a court of inquiry if it looks like a national crisis. These special inquiries report to Parliament and hence to the public, while the committees do not. The inquiry and investigation procedure is not a means of threatening disputants with the majesty of the law, but a way of exposing the facts behind a dispute and making the issues clear.

The recent history of industrial arbitration has been confused by the survival into peace time of wartime regulations, such as

D

the Employment and National Arbitration Order, 1940, which became notorious as Order 1305, its serial number as a Statutory Rule and Order. It ran until 1951, and was the occasion of a public prosecution by a Labour Attorney-General, Sir Hartley (now Lord) Shawcross, of a group of dockworkers who had called a strike in contravention of the order. The prosecution had ultimately to be dropped. But the effect on trade union opinion of the survival into peace of compulsory arbitration and anti-strike legislation compelled the drafting of a compromise measure, the Industrial Disputes Order, 1951, known as Order 1376 and also deriving its authority from Defence Regulations.

Under this Order a new Industrial Disputes Tribunal replaced Order 1305's National Arbitration Tribunal, and continued to administer compulsory arbitration awards, although it could not prohibit strikes or lock-outs. This Tribunal was wound up in 1959 after some two years of discussion in the National Joint Advisory Council. It has not been replaced, but under the Terms and Conditions of Employment Act, 1959, employers and workers have a statutory right to call upon the Industrial Court to adjudicate in cases where some breach of the set conditions of employment in an industry seems to be taking place. This is called the claims procedure. Order 1376 would have called a claim an 'issue', while to Order 1305 it would have been a 'question'. Procedure and nomenclature play a large part in official negotiations, and seem as forbidding to the outsider as legal jargon. Most workers and some managers who are not engaged in labour relations work may have found the official institutions of dispute settlement difficult to follow and to remember. Lack of clear understanding of the voluntary machinery and of the stages of arbitration probably accounts for some of the unofficial actions taken by impatient shop-floor workers who have tired of waiting for something decisive to happen, and cannot help feeling that the lengthy procedures are a 'guv'nors' technique for postponing action. Their official paid representatives in the union know in detail the collective bargaining apparatus for their particular industry. The rank and file union member, on the whole, does not. A cursory look at the tangle of voluntary and statutory negotiating committees and councils quickly reveals that this is a specialist field of study.

First, there are three groups of joint negotiating arrangements; one has evolved in private enterprise, one in the nationalized industries and a third in the public service (both central and local). Secondly, in the private sector each industry has a different pattern of negotiating committees and procedures, and some industries, like engineering, are extremely complex. Engineering would, in fact, embrace ironfounding, machine tools and vehicle manufacture, but there are subdivisions, such as cablemaking and nut, screw and bolt manufacture which have their own negotiating machinery. There are, in engineering, the federated companies, i.e. those that are members of the Engineering and Allied Employers' National Federation, and the non-federated or non-member firms. The latter for the most part take their guidance on wage payments and rates from the bargains arrived at by the Federation and even pursue in their negotiations similar procedures that have been separately agreed with the unions.

The Federation, as its name implies, is a combination of local associations dealing with various branches of the engineering industry. It has between four and five thousand member companies with an aggregate employment of some two million workers. Its opposite number on the trade union's side is the Confederation of Shipbuilding and Engineering Unions (the Shipbuilding Employers' Federation by contrast is a separate body from the Engineering Employers Federation) with about forty member unions of which the largest is the Amalgamated Engineering Union. The members of the AEU are drawn from all grades of workers in the industry, from the highly skilled to the unskilled. Other unions in the Confederation, however, are organized more as craft unions, like the patternmakers and boilermakers. The picture is further confused by the fact that a great many workers in the engineering industry are organized by the general unions, like the Transport and General Workers' Union and the National Union of General and Municipal Workers, while clerical and administrative staffs tend to belong to the Clerical and Administrative Workers' union or to no union at all. Draughtsmen are again separately organized in the Draughtsmen's and Allied Trades Association.

According to the *Industrial Relations Handbook* it has become customary for the Confederation to approach the employers on a matter of national negotiation in relation to pay, hours, holidays, shift working and the like and to invite them to a conference at which a case is presented. Matters affecting only one union, like the electricians, are left to the union to raise with the Federation. After hearing the workers' case the employers go away and consider it, then pronounce their opinion or make an offer at a second conference. This continues until agreement is reached or the negotiations break down. 'There is no agreed procedure to deal with the latter eventuality', adds the *Handbook*, 'and should the unions decide to press the case, they may seek conciliation or arbitration, or take direct industrial action.' They may, in a word, strike. One may reflect upon this complex procedure and come to the conclusion that it has two weaknesses. It is cumbersome and slow (which some may argue is a good thing nationally as it postpones the danger of direct action); and it can lead eventually to strike action.

Within companies in the engineering industry there are agreed procedures, laid down in 1922 and revised in 1955, but not all the unions affiliated to the Confederation are signatories to this agreement, while some unions are although they are not affiliated. The basic formula guiding the primary moves in a dispute or grievance is that the employers 'have the right to manage' while the unions 'have the right to exercise their functions'. Tribute is paid to consultation as a means of avoiding disputes, and provision is made for joint committees of shop stewards and management representatives to be set up. The appointment of shop stewards, being largely a union matter, has become general, with some companies extending special privileges, including training, to them. But the projected joint committees, being more a matter for management action motivated by desire for such consultation presumably, have failed to materialize.

Based on the shop steward system there is what American managers would call a grievance procedure, whereby a worker with a matter to raise must first of all approach his foreman, on the understanding that if he fails to receive satisfaction he may then ask his shop steward to raise it with the next line of management, the senior foreman or superintendent, followed by a works conference if necessary, all the way up to a central conference of the union officials, via the employer's office and a local conference of union officials and management representatives. There are many variants of this procedure, but basically this is the pattern in engineering, with other arrangements on behalf of other unions, like DATA or the Association of Scientific Workers.

This exhaustive agreement between employers and unions in this industry, complete with manual workers' wage rates for both time and piece rates, suggests that here is one solution to the disputes problem. But many in the engineering industry would acknowledge that in practice this complicated set of arrangements does not seem to work, with employers paying 'over the odds' in many sectors of the industry, either by means of allowed overtime or in some other way that does not conflict with the federation's rules, and with unions pressing for concessions of this kind, such as the shorter working week, which is a means of creating further overtime.

It also has to be remembered that the collective bargaining structure in Britain is voluntary and therefore that it is perfectly possible for companies to remain outside the system and pursue somewhat different practices to those normal to the industry. Companies have been known to boast that they were not involved with the unions because their rates were so high that even trade union members who were recruited failed to keep up their membership on the grounds that it was now unnecessary.

There is the added difficulty that today power on the shop floor resides with the shop stewards (see Chapter VI), who are on the whole untrained, except in a handful of cases. Some unions have the money and the will to undertake shop steward training, but if it is done through independent organizations, such as the Industrial Society, the employers are usually expected to foot the bill on the grounds that it redounds to their benefit.

There is the additional difficulty that actual trade union power today does not reside in the formal authority of the union official. Indeed there is an almost inverse relationship between actual power and formal authority, in that the further one rises above the shop floor the more does union authority become tenuous and unreal. Power, unquestionably in these times of full employment, is vested in the leaders at the place of work and it is here that training and development for the exercise and control of this power is most scanty and least understood. Most shop stewards have not received one hour of formal training from either the company that employs them or the union that uses them. They are plunged, often the least unwilling conscripts for the task, into a situation where their power is often equal to or greater than that of the plant manager—and they rarely receive even an atom of guidance or education for the task.

After election, it is true that some stewards can attend shop stewards' courses organized by their unions and in some other cases by the more progressive firms. But the proportion attending is lamentably small compared to the size and scope of the problem. Most unions have neither the money, the time nor the staff to meet this problem, while others even lack the inclination. The feeling is still all too widespread that the best classroom is the shop floor and the appropriate university the branch meeting-room.

The problem becomes compounded by the reliance that the ordinary worker places on personal leadership. He looks, naturally, for leadership from the employer or the employer's representative, for it is here that the decisions over engagement or dismissal are made. It is management that pays the wages and issues the orders and is paid itself to display leadership. It is natural then to look for leadership from this quarter and when, for any reason, it does not flow from the expected quarter, then expectation gives way to derision and contempt and the worker turns to other leaders—the shop stewards. There is, in fact, no reason why these two power sources should not positively coalesce and discharge their functions within agreed boundaries, but it is more often the case that the shop steward becomes established by more negative processes—a failure by management; adoption of new leadership from shop stewards; resistance by management; retreat by management then abdication.

Gradually the worker comes to feel that the solutions to *his* problems (and these after all are the most important problems in his world) can only be sought through the shop steward, who begins to acquire more real power with the worker than the manager, the director or even the national official of the very union to which he belongs. The latter must often seem to the man on the shop floor as someone even more remote than the plant manager. Preoccupied as he is with the ridiculous gavotte of national wage-bargaining or with the endless round of committees, courts, conferences, and all the other extra-mural irrelevancies with which the unions have surrounded themselves in the last twenty to thirty years, he must often appear to the ordinary member as almost a being from another world. And well he might be, for he has no time or opportunity to concern himself with the vital considerations of the workplace.

What occurs at high level is out of focus for the man on the assembly line or at the workbench. His real loyalties lie nearer home. Managers would do well to remember both this, which is an obvious fact that somehow escapes full attention in the working situation, and the idea that central wage-fixing by high-level bargaining has come to seem to the rank-and-file union member as remote and god-given as the Budget that puts a penny on the pint. If these outline facts are borne in mind, the phenomenon of the unofficial strike or stoppage as it tends to be called ceases to appear quite so mysterious or even unreasonable. Men do like to have some say in their own destinies.

Private industry has evolved a tangle of complicated procedures for settling wages, hours and conditions of work in nearly every sector, from the docks to the theatre. In the last twenty years, with the sharp increase in nationalization that came with the first post-war Labour Government, there has also had to be a bargaining structure created for the publicly operated industries. As some of these were taken over by the State under a Labour administration they sometimes had trade unionists nominated to their Boards, with the result that they often encountered most carefully drafted national conciliation schemes, as the Coal Board had based on the old employer-union agreements, but going all the way down to the individual pit via the district. Gas and electricity have national joint industrial councils, as does air transport, while the British Railways Board negotiates at top level with the Railway Staff National Council. The railways, after all, have only three unions to deal with, the National Union of Railwaymen, the Amalgamated Society of Locomotive Engineers and Firemen (the 'footplatemen') and the Transport Salaried Staffs' Association. It is almost a one-union industry, and there have been times when it would have benefited from being so. But there are also craft unions involved, in the railway workshops for example, and as the railways modernize both the Electrical Trades Union and the Amalgamated Engineering Union play a more important part. Merely because an industry is nationalized, contrary to what is commonly assumed, labour relations are not automatically made simpler.

The third area where joint negotiating machinery has been set up or has evolved is in Government and local government service. It is a sensitive area, for obvious reasons, especially when trade unionism takes hold among an organization like the police. After the General Strike of 1926 the Government of the day passed a Trade Disputes Act barring civil servants from organizing themselves into trade unions affiliated to the Trades Union Congress, but this did not effectively prevent the ramifications of unionism in civil service departments like the General Post Office. Generally speaking the civil service bargaining structure rests upon the Whitley Council basis worked out after the First World War. It has since been modified to fit changed conditions, just as the Burnham Committee structure has been developed to handle the education side, which grew mightily after 1918. As far as this book is concerned, however, public service negotiating machinery is less relevant than the private industry bargaining systems that concern managers in their daily work.

It has become customary to leave much of the preliminary bargaining and negotiating to the personnel or labour relations executives in the larger companies. And when the negotiations reach the highest levels the specialists in the employers' organizations take over on behalf of their member companies. For these reasons, among others, line managers tend to be shut off from first-hand experience of the bargaining procedure and atmosphere. This is not altogether a good thing, either for them or their companies. An awareness of the labour relations world and its nuances is a valuable additional asset for any manager, because it restores to him the meaningful part of management, which is the managing of people.

Line management, because of the segregation of the personnel or labour relations function, has gradually become in the larger firm the management of things—machines, money and materials. Even the marketing side of management, which has most to do with people as customers, is inclined to treat them as statistics to be compiled, analysed and exploited. General managers themselves have in many companies come to depend on their personnel advisers to solve the problems that have to do with people. Technical managers will happily relinquish this part of their control to the specialists. The consequence is that many line managers have increasingly been left out of personnel work and have thus ceased to be true managers. It has been said that all line managers should be able to be their own personnel managers and that the personnel manager's job is to work himself out of one. The truth of the matter at present in Britain seems to be that the line manager has grown too accustomed to having little or nothing to do with the whole range of personnel work. It now seems to be a large additional burden on top of his other duties. And he has been taught little or nothing about its complexities during his formal training or education.

When one considers the weaknesses that beset British industry at this time—overmanning, excessive overtime working, systematic soldiering (spinning the job out unnecessarily), restrictive practices, demarcation and interunion disputes, absenteeism, low productivity per worker and unofficial strikes —it is apparent that the gap between managerial thinking and the attitudes of workpeople has closed very little, if at all, over the years. The handful of productivity bargains that have been struck in three oil companies, the electricity industry, British Oxygen and Pressed Steel, all handled incidentally by the personnel departments for the most part, indicates a possible way ahead, though a slow and painful one. The methods and some of the results are examined in Chapter VIII and Appendix 1. The history of such agreements suggests that, initially, there is a deeply rooted suspicion on the part of trade unions and their members of these approaches from management. Once this is recognized, as at Esso's Fawley refinery, it ceases to be quite as dangerous. To pretend, however, that this not unnatural suspicion does not exist, or to contend that it should not and is therefore unreasonable, is to put a foot wrong at the outset of any negotiations. There are two sides to industry and it is no good behaving as if this were not so.

The paragraphs above, sketchy though they may be compared with the detailed and complicated descriptions in the *Industrial Relations Handbook* and in the welter of official literature relating to each separate industry, serve to demonstrate how the basic differences between management and workers can be handled formally. Looking at the collective bargaining machinery dispassionately it has all the appearance of a series of fortifications built up between the contending parties in industry. The larger and more centralized that industry becomes, the higher and more impenetrable become the fortifications. They can hardly be described seriously as channels of communication, if in fact they were ever regarded as any such thing.

However, once a mechanism of this kind is set up it has to have things to do. A bureaucracy does not easily accept that its mountains are in reality molehills. The long-term solution must be to simplify bargaining procedures. The short-term solution ought to be to keep small differences small, in the hands of the managers and the local officials or shop stewards, and not to permit them to be blown up into proportions that require the attention of the national councils and committees. That will be achieved only when line management takes the personnel element of its job to heart.

CHAPTER VI

THE SHOP STEWARDS

THE shop steward has become the bogeyman of industrial relations in the public eye. But for him employers, managers and responsible trade union officers could contract their bargains and settle their differences. There he is, it seems, a necessary evil, in close and influential touch with the shop floor (he is after all one of the shop-floor team) and inclined to see things parochially instead of in terms of broad and sweeping policy. The way some ill-informed comment is phrased creates the misleading impression that all shop stewards are saboteurs, if not Communists.

This reputation probably derives from their popularly supposed origin in engineering factories during the First World War, whereas in fact the Amalgamated Engineering Union passed a resolution in 1878 empowering its District Committees to appoint stewards, according to the union's official historian Dr James Jeffreys in *The Story of the Engineers*.[1] The so-called Shop Stewards' Movement is associated with the First World War and the labour troubles on Clydeside. But even William Gallacher himself, lifelong Communist and self-styled agitator on the Clyde in those days, says in his autobiography that, as an official of a craft union merged into the AEU, he reported what he considered to be the shortcomings of his fellow-officials to the shop stewards, 'and thus it reached the factories and branch meetings'.[2]

It was the war that boosted the appointment of stewards in the engineering factories. Until 1914 and after they had not been numerous. As Jeffreys says, they had been recognized in the AEU's 1896 rules 'as having a function in the Society (the Amalgamated Society of Engineers), but for many years they were unknown outside Scotland and Belfast, and their functions

[1] 1945, p. 137.　　[2] *The Revolt on the Clyde*, 1936, p. 33.

were limited to ensuring that members remained in benefit and that newcomers were Society men'. In the printing industry they had their counterparts in the local official known as the Father of the Chapel or FOC. But other industries acquired these shop-floor organizers and dues-collectors or their equivalents during and after the Second World War. The shop steward's rather mixed reputation as revolutionary and 'wild-cat-strike provoker' is far from deserved, therefore, and is based on a few misunderstood anecdotes dating back about half a century. The sparse references to them in union histories show that they were brought into being as a vital link between the district offices and the workers in the factories, particularly at times when the number of newcomers to manufacturing industry was constantly increasing. This helps to explain the sharp rise in the appointment of stewards in both wars, when the engineering industry was heavily 'diluted' with unskilled labour.

The real importance of the shop steward to his trade union is that he is quite simply the man on the spot, the point of contact between the union and its members. As such he is, naturally, chosen by his fellow-workers, but the procedure that governs his election, his relations with the salaried union officers and with the employers at his place of work differs from one industry to another.

However, his duties are nearly always the same. He is expected to act as a recruiting agent, sometimes to collect subscriptions, to issue the union's literature and instructions, to represent the workers to management and sit on any committees that are set up to bring together either management and workers, union and members, or shop stewards of one union and another. In an industry, like motor manufacture, where more than twenty unions are involved, he may be a member of a joint shop stewards' committee the object of which is to try to co-ordinate disputes procedures and problems and other labour relations matters. He is seldom if ever paid for his work, but in some companies he is allowed time during the working day to perform his duties. In some companies there has been considerable reluctance to pay a shop-floor worker a wage merely for carrying out the instructions of his union. Equally, in some unions there has been a reluctance to let too much power and influence accumulate in the hands of the shop-floor representative.

The automatic association in the public mind of shop stewards with unofficial action is in part a product of this dual objection to their strong tactical position. Managements tacitly try to limit its influence by routeing grievance procedures through the foreman in the first instance. Trade unionists have remarked that this arrangement can place unions and workers at a disadvantage in negotiation. The Trades Union Congress General Council has recorded its view that it creates a situation in which 'if workers want a change to which the managers object they must go without until the procedure is exhausted: but if the managers want a change to which the workers object the change stays while the procedure is being gone through'.[1]

Management's response to this criticism is fairly standard. The task of management is to manage, to run the business. It would be wrong, therefore, to detract from the authority of first-line management, the foreman or supervisor, by allowing workers to take their grievances in the first instance to their shop stewards. The foremen themselves, who have long suffered the unenviable experience of being ground between the upper millstone of management and the nether millstone of the unions, would probably take the management line of thinking on shop-floor relations, both to preserve their own position and because they see their job as controller of the shop-floor teams in their charge. The shop steward, it has been argued in opposition to this attitude, only takes over in these circumstances when the foreman fails to respond adequately to the needs of workers under his control. The argument generally goes on to recommend training for both foremen and stewards. Indeed, there have been experiments in training them together, particularly in human relations subjects, but without notable results. The dominant factors will always be the working situation and the basic policy of the company.

This is not to say that foremanship training and the training of shop stewards are not good things. To expect mature workers to accept promotion and responsibility and then not to help them acquire the essential skills to support them is shortsighted. It is possibly less of a human relations problem for the shop steward, for he starts off with the official approbation and support of his fellow-workers, while the foremen has some resistance to overcome and acceptance to win. Also he is not necessarily as

[1] Jenkins and Mortimer, *British Trade Unions To-day*, 1965, p. 12.

familiar with the outlook and customs of the unions with which he will have to deal as the shop steward is almost certain to be. Most foremen begin their careers on the shop floor, but not all of them take an interest in the intricacies of unionism. Indeed, on occasion they may adopt an unsympathetic political attitude, which will not apparently interfere with their work but eventually emerges as a recognition by the shop-floor workers that this particular supervisor is an opponent rather than an ally. All such considerations bear thinking about when industrial relations in the workplace are under scrutiny.

It is important to look at the role of the shop steward not only as a key function in workplace relations, because of his ready acceptance by union members, and because he is the foreman's opposite number, but as a union function that is becoming increasingly important in modern industry. As Jenkins and Mortimer point out in their book, 'The focal point of trade union interest has shifted to a considerable extent from the branch room to the factory. Only fairly severe unemployment would be likely, temporarily, to check this trend.' When two senior officials of two white-collar unions (respectively ASSET and DATA, the supervisors and the draughtsmen) feel this to be true, we can be reasonably certain that it is. But why should it be so?

Arthur Marsh, a lecturer in industrial relations, has attempted to explain the increased importance of workplace bargaining and union activity as a process of 'filling in' the details left unstated in industry-wide agreements which lay down certain minima, including rates of pay, shift-working conditions, overtime premiums, holidays and the length of the working week. But such agreements seldom include what are often more immediate matters for the shop floor—worker engagement and dismissal procedure, methods and times of payment and detailed hours of work.[1] As long as industry-wide bargaining overlooks such matters there will be a tendency to settle them at the place of work. The 'Blue Book' produced by the Esso Petroleum Company's management as a preliminary to the Fawley bargaining (see Appendix 1) was a detailed document aimed primarily at the refinery shop stewards, who received it with a mixture of apprehension, dislike and acceptance, according

---

[1] *Managers and Shop Stewards* (Institute of Personnel Management), 1963, pp. 13–17.

to which craft union they represented and how they viewed the extent of the concessions that would be expected of them. As Allan Flanders pointed out in his official study of the Fawley agreements, here was a plant where relations between management and stewards were already good, even if the stewards themselves were wary of 'playing management's game', in the sense of allowing management to undermine their authority with their members by seizing the bargaining initiative.

Flanders also pointed out that the productivity agreements concluded at Fawley underline the important trend towards workplace bargaining in industry. At Fawley there were even union officials who found themselves dependent for guidance upon their local chief stewards. The increasing power of the shop stewards, as evinced at Fawley, may therefore be seen as part of a general trend away from industry-wide bargaining and in favour of plant bargaining, although so far it is no more than that, few companies outside the oil industry and electricity supply having pursued it.[1]

One probable explanation for this trend is stated in the opening of this chapter. As trade unionism has increased and full employment reinforced the scope of collective bargaining more and more employers and Trade Union Officers have sought to contain this process within the confines of centrally negotiated agreements. They have tried to control an industry from the centre, thus creating first apathy, then action, at the periphery.

This has simultaneously deprived branches and districts of the importance they once enjoyed when settlements were made at those levels. There are still industries in which local agreements survive. In the cotton industry, for example, there are district lists of piecework rates and the local officials are expected, by both management and workers, to deal personally with on-the-spot union affairs, which leaves little or no scope for workshop bargains or for the workshop representatives to increase their influence.

In most industries, however, there are general industry-wide agreements, broadly drafted and leaving plenty of scope for 'filling in' and even for local disputes. Indeed, disputes have helped to establish workplace bargaining in some industries. Marsh points out that, in addition, managements have reinforced the shop stewards in their accretion of power by

[1] *The Fawley Productivity Agreements*, 1964, p. 112 et seq., pp. 201–3.

refusing to concede detailed regulation from outside of work-shop conditions or to admit full-time union officials to their factories. Managements have been inclined to regard the practical detail of bargains as an invasion of the prerogatives at the place of work, and look upon union visiting as tantamount to another version of factory inspection, but by persons lacking the requisite authority.[1]

Marsh goes on to point out that, because grievance procedures, which are essential to good works relations, have tended to evolve into bargaining systems, they have undermined the influence of works councils and committees. These institutions of joint consultation (see Chapter X) have generally been conducted in such a way as to avoid economic questions, these being regarded as outside their terms of reference. Naturally, therefore, where the national bargaining seemed defective, work groups have looked for leadership to their elected representative, the shop steward. In addition, it is difficult to draw a line between one subject of consultation and another in order to decide whether it is admissible at the works council. There is no such hesitation among the stewards.

The upshot of this arbitrary role that stewards are called upon to play, impelled by the group pressures on them in the workplace, is that they enjoy a doubly influential position. As Flanders puts it: 'As spokesmen of work groups in the enterprise, they may participate in the making of internal rules either separately or jointly with management. As representatives of their union they have a responsibility for enforcing its rules or the agreements that it has entered into with employers.' They are even able to make or amend internal rules without seeking the approval of the union authorities.[2]

From the union point of view the shop steward or his equivalent is a voluntary official, whose activity is a welcome reinforcement of the work of the full-time officers who, in many unions, are not numerous enough to cope with the welter of day-to-day business. Without this voluntary assistance many unions would be in a weak position as far as service to their members was concerned. If the leadership is to maintain any pretence of close contact and awareness of members' feelings it cannot afford to dispense with the workshop representative.

[1] Marsh, *op. cit.*, pp. 13–14.
[2] *Industrial Relations: what is wrong with the system?* (I.P.M.), 1965, p. 16.

Most unions have to deal with anything from 3,000 to 4,000 members to each salaried officer, and to staff themselves up to the point where this figure could be significantly reduced they might have to raise subscriptions to a level that most members would be unwilling to pay. It seems, therefore, that the shop steward will remain a part of the industrial relations scene for a long time yet and will therefore need to be accepted more readily by management.

There is another aspect to this consolidation of the position of stewards that has not escaped the notice of some wide-awake managers. As amateurs in negotiation, until they acquire some experience or receive some training, shop stewards are doubly vulnerable, for they are also the paid employees of the company and not of the union. A number of unions have noted this uneasily, for they realize that confronted with experienced managers their shop stewards are liable to be too conciliatory on occasions, or too naïve. Alan Fox, in his history of the National Union of Boot and Shoe Operatives, records a trade unionist as saying that he fears that shop committees will consist of some men 'whom the employer can squeeze. If an employer, through his representatives, is smooth tongued, our men will give way every time'.[1]

Since the time referred to by Fox, shop stewards have become better educated, and are more likely to be sceptical than gullible nowadays. Indeed, there is some justification in thinking that they are too inclined to be suspicious of management. But like all such attitudes in labour relations this suspicion has its roots in the treatment meted out to such men in the past. Once bitten, twice shy is not, as far as we know, the slogan of any particular union, but the movement could well adopt it as its own.

If one takes into account the inevitable fact that, as far as the shop-floor worker is concerned, the shop steward is all that he ever sees of his union, especially as branch meetings are notoriously ill attended, being on the whole dull, formal and at a time of day when working men want to rest and relax, it becomes clear that willy-nilly the steward possesses a leadership position. It is not surprising that some trade union officers have shown themselves worried about this, partly because of uneasy recollections of the National Shop Stewards' Movement and partly because it has seemed natural enough to some stewards to

[1] Cited in Marsh, *op. cit.*, p. 19.

E

organize themselves either on a multi-union plant basis (shop stewards' committees) or even on a national basis for the purpose of meeting together for an annual conference. These tendencies the trade unions have firmly resisted, on the grounds that shop stewards, being militant unionists (the effort called for in such voluntary work and the exposed position in the eyes of the employers demands and gets resolute volunteers) are almost certain to have advanced political views, even extreme opinions. They might therefore, in separately constituted organizations, become a prey to 'disruptive political influences', to use official phraseology, meaning Communist or Trotskyite pressures.

The unions, therefore, are only too keen to integrate their shop stewards as closely into their structure as possible, and one or two unions have revised their rules accordingly. There is a difficulty, however, apart from the general inertia associated with the revision of union rules, and that is the part that management has to play. The steward is the point of contact most of the time between union and employer. If his status is to be changed to suit union policy it will inevitably affect his status at his place of work. Management should have a say in the nature of any such change. This is easy to state, but far from easy to implement.

It almost goes without saying that anything that employers could do to strengthen workshop representation must, in the long term, improve local relations. By supporting their employees' elected representatives they may feel that they are offering hostages to fortune. In fact, they would be demonstrating confidence in their employees' responsibility. In most cases there are grounds for believing that this could evoke a satisfactory response, as the familiar and traditional managerial approach to workplace bargaining has shown itself as intolerant and reluctant, employers preferring to negotiate with union officials outside the factory, even when experience has demonstrated the possibility of achieving speedy on-the-spot settlements over a wide range of minor, and even a few major, points of dispute. Had shop stewards been more acceptable in the eyes of their unions, as well as by managements, such negotiations might have been more successful and therefore widespread. As it is, there has developed a strong tendency for stewards to 'go it alone' and indulge in what their union leaders apostrophize as 'unofficial action'.

The strong emergence of workplace bargaining and the key role in it of the unpaid union representative is a modern industrial phenomenon that managements would do well to recognize and handle systematically, as one or two outstandingly intelligent companies have already begun to do. To adopt an inflexible, out-of-date attitude to 'unofficial' developments of this nature is not merely unconstructive, it is unwise. As long as the main elements of union-management agreements are preserved or changed only through mutually acceptable procedures, there seems to be no reason why plant bargaining should not take place, given the approval of the unions whose members are involved. Certainly it gives practical and fruitful recognition to what appears to be an inevitable state of affairs, the direct confrontation of shop stewards and managers. Also it demonstrates the myopia of those benevolent critics of the industrial relations scene who would attempt (and vainly as far as the historical evidence may be taken as an indication) to abolish the 'two sides of industry'.

In prevailing circumstances in British industry there are two sides. Call them capital and labour, if you will, although this pair of words carries a special and not entirely helpful emphasis. Call them labour and management. But whatever vocabulary is selected, two sides or sets of interests there are, at this moment in time, and on the whole they are differing interests. When orators declaim their criticisms of trade unions they generally bring in a phrase or two about wanting more pay for less work. Work is capable of a multitude of definitions and is not necessarily to be measured in terms of hours worked. Any old soldier will confirm that a long 'working' day can be so organized as to produce no tangible results at all. But there is something in the rhetorical charge. For the bargaining of organized labour over the century and a half of its existence in British industry has undoubtedly accomplished two things: it has obtained improvements for its adherents; and it has put employers on their mettle. Cheap labour makes for technically retarded industries.

There is a further practical matter: Why do managements assume that a workers' representative, when he reports back to his constituents, will be accurate, convincing or enthusiastic? This mundane consideration should not be allowed to elude managers who would like to put consultation into practice.

Unless they can somehow make certain that the workers' representatives will have the desire, the ability and the time to convey the conclusions of the meeting to their workmates (and be able to answer the inevitable questions), they would probably do better not to hold the meeting at all.

The conflict between shop floor and management has its constructive aspect, and as long as managers and shop stewards, backed by their unions, recognize this, progress can still be made.

CHAPTER VII

RESTRICTIVE PRACTICES IN AN AGE OF AFFLUENCE

THE legacy of traditional attitudes to work and responsibility on both sides of industry, no matter how justified in the past, is probably the greatest single cause of the average, and in some cases lower than average, performance by British management and organized workers alike. In current discussions about restrictive practices, attention is rightly concentrated on the 'labour' aspects of the problem rather than on the contribution that 'management' makes to it. This is not to say that the restrictive practices of management—a propensity for price-fixing; limitation of output; resistance to change and many others—are more worthy than their labour counterparts, or less injurious to expansion and economic growth. It is rather due to the widespread belief that management restrictive practices are more readily contained and modified than is the case with those operated by workers and their unions. The fact that experience has all too frequently shown this belief to be naïve, and the further fact that management has revealed a capacity for subtly extending and maintaining its own practices, in a way that would excite the envy of the more conservative trade unionists, has not materially affected the emphasis within the area of the debate. And, of course, it is true that management is more vulnerable and, *ipso facto*, its practices more amenable to modification than are those of an army of work-people. Management is exposed to the sanctions of its own executives; to economic forces and to the power of the legislature in a way that labour is not. It is for this reason that the use of legislation to compel greater efficiency in industry has been concentrated against management rather than labour in recent years. The experience of the nineteenth century, with the attempts to outlaw trades unionism or to condemn them as being in restraint of trade, demonstrated the futility of legislation as an adequate instrument to regulate the behaviour of labour. In more recent years the ineffectiveness in peace-time of the Conditions of Employment and National Arbitration Order (1305) and the Industrial Disputes Order (1376) are further examples of the limitations to which legislation is exposed.

It is not surprising, therefore, that in the realm of restrictive practices, Parliament has not refrained from interfering with the rights and freedoms of employers under the Monopolies and Restrictive Practices Acts, but has, so far, not ventured to interfere (apart from the defunct Trade Disputes Act 1927 and the now withdrawn Orders previously mentioned) with the practices, restrictive or otherwise, of trade unions as such. As recently as 1959 a White Paper on 'Practices Impeding the Full and Efficient Use of Manpower' asserted that proposals[1] (currently under active discussion) for bringing the restrictive practices of workmen within the framework of the law would not be effective, and it went on to urge that such difficulties were more likely to be resolved through the joint consideration of industry itself.

But efforts by industry to resolve these problems have not been noticeably successful—at least on the scale that is required to sustain the growth targets suggested by the NEDC and in the National Plan upon which the 'Age of Affluence' depends. The publicity that surrounded the Fawley and Linwood experiments, and the readiness with which large sections of industry and government hailed these experiments as breakthroughs in the search for greater productivity, is a measure of the lack of progress and the inertia that inhibits positive action in this field. If these examples were other than rarities in British industrial experience, our record of production and productivity would not compare so unfavourably with other industrial nations.

The problem that confronts British industry is not so much the realization that increasing productivity depends on harnessing the goodwill of labour, but on developing in management the determination to take positive action about it. There has been no lack of readiness, in post-war years, to recognize

---

[1] E.g. by a Conservative Party organization, that workmen or unions operating restrictive practices should have the responsibility of satisfying the Restrictive Practices Court that such behaviour was in the public interest.

that the power of 'the sack' has diminished along with mass unemployment. Or to recognize that the power of organized labour has grown until it has equalled, or indeed surpassed, that of management. But, all too often, this recognition has been accompanied by a feeling of impotence on the part of management. The belief that 'the unions will never agree to it' (whenever 'it' involves any change for the better) is reinforced by an unwillingness—particularly by line management—to become involved in labour relations at all. 'Management' tends to be understood by managers as the 'management of things rather than people' and the tedious interruptions of work by labour disputes or restrictions are best left to the personnel managers, and to the union officials. It is a curious paradox of our industrial life that so many managers accept full responsibility for the introduction of new techniques: for the development of new products: for the securing of new outlets, and indeed for change in all other aspects of industrial life, except that of labour—where the greatest potential for advancement undoubtedly exists! Estimates made in Britain of potential increases in output vary between 25 per cent and a 50 per cent increase due to attitude alone. One consultant[1] has described as 'explosive' the increase in productivity that is latent in the attitude of workers. He has further suggested that if, in the next generation, we can make the supreme effort to understand human attitudes better, this of itself could contribute more to productivity than improved technology. And the present authors see no reason to believe that such a prophecy is necessarily exaggerated. One fact stands out more clearly than anything else—the almost limitless ingenuity of workmen, either individually or collectively, to devise better ways of performing the tasks imposed on them by management. It is a belief that has been fulfilled many times in those years in spite of the touching faith that managers have placed, from time to time, upon so-called scientific systems of work measurement. The basis of conflict, rather than co-operation, that is inherent in most of these systems[2] ensures that the worker sees his interests as being different from those of the enterprise as a whole, and sets in train a process of thought and behaviour that will invariably leave a reservoir of capacity virtually untapped.

[1] Peter Drucker, *The New Society*, 1951.
[2] The Scanlon and Rucker plans are probably the most significant exceptions.

Yet these workmen are the same people who at other times follow pursuits that are not only unrewarding (i.e. in a financial sense) but are expensive, arduous, uncomfortable, disagreeable and dirty. How is it that industry, which provides workmen with the levels on which they fix the standards of life for themselves and their families, is regarded by them as a burden? Why do they imperil these living standards by irksome and outdated restrictions? And why bring to the pursuit of those standards much less enthusiasm than they devote to vegetable gardening; to running boy's clubs; to watching football matches in the most impossible weather conditions; to repairing obsolete motor-cars; to canvassing for political parties; to sitting for endless hours, in cold and damp by depressing rivers and canals, angling for rare and inedible fish?

The traditional management answer to this conundrum has usually been—at least in post-war years—to seek a financial solution in the belief that the only valid human motive for work is gain. But, as Dr J. A. C. Brown has said[1]: 'The belief that money is the sole, or even the most important of several motives for work, is so foolish that anyone who seriously holds this opinion is thereby rendered incapable of understanding industry or the industrial worker'.

Dr Brown's work, and that of other sociologists from Elton Mayo to Douglas McGregor, have demonstrated that what the worker demands from his labour is not merely, or even mainly, higher pay and shorter hours but greater understanding of the purpose and result of his labours. He seeks, generally quite unconsciously, increased participation and an 'ownership' (as Drucker calls it) or control of his labour. Money, after a certain point, becomes one of the lesser stimuli and is supplemented by other needs for which his behaviour becomes a continuing expression. The need for significance and the security and well-being that goes with it.

Against this background the retention of restrictive practices assumes different proportions and the complaint of managers, that this behaviour has lost all possible justification as a protective device in conditions of full employment, is a meaningless irrelevance. The restrictive practice developed in times of unemployment to increase security became, as unemployment decreased, an artifice for increasing remuneration. Then, as

[1] *The Social Psychology of Industry*, 1954.

both these objectives were realized and maintained, a point of satiety over money needs produced, not an abandonment of these practices but their retention—to advance leisure: to reflect the independence of the worker *vis à vis* management: to increase his significance: to emphasize *his* control over *his* efforts: to oppose his power against the traditional power of management. To achieve these things and perhaps many more, and to achieve them, moreover, without any clear appreciation by the worker what it is that he is seeking to achieve. He may, in fact, vigorously assert that restrictive practices are still defensive tactics to protect his security or his craft or his wage packet, when at bottom he knows that these rights are in no danger. He may still claim to be defending some battle that has long been decided in his favour, when in reality he is dimly endeavouring to give expression to a whole new series of wants, that he may be quite unaware of, but are nonetheless real for all that. As McGregor has put it[1]: 'Human needs are organized in a series of levels—a hierarchy of importance. At the lowest level, but pre-eminent in importance when they are thwarted, are the physiological needs. Man lives by bread alone, when there is no bread. Unless the circumstances are unusual, his needs for love, for status, for recognition are inoperative when his stomach has been empty for a while. But when he eats regularly and adequately, hunger ceases to be an important need. . . . The same is true of the other physiological needs of man—for rest, exercise, shelter, protection from the elements.'

A satisfied need is not a motivator of behaviour! This is a fact of profound significance.

When the physiological needs are reasonably satisfied, needs at the next higher level begin to dominate man's behaviour—to motivate him. These are the safety needs, for protection against the danger of deprivation. Some people mistakenly refer to these as needs for security. However, unless man is in a dependent relationship where he fears arbitrary deprivation, he does not demand security. The need is for the 'fairest possible break'. When he is confident of this, he is more willing to take risks. But when he feels threatened or dependent, his greatest need is for protection, and for security.

The fact needs little emphasis that since every industrial employee is in at least a partially dependent relationship, security

[1] *The Human Side of Enterprise.*

anxieties may assume considerable importance. Arbitrary management actions (behaviour which arouses uncertainty with respect to continued employment or which reflects favouritism or discrimination, unpredictable administration of policy) can be powerful motivators of the safety needs in the employment relationship at every level from worker to vice-president. When man's physiological needs are satisfied and he is no longer fearful about his physical welfare, his social needs become important motivators of his behaviour. These are such needs as those for belonging, for association, for acceptance by one's fellows, for giving and receiving friendship.

It is when restrictive practices are looked at in this way, as the outward expression of a multiplicity of needs that are socio-logical as well as physiological that the manager can begin to see the possibility of solutions. This is the beginning. The real-ization that though a particular restriction may, in fact, be truly a reflection of a demand for more money, it may equally well be nothing of the kind. This point may still be true even though the worker himself represents his dissatisfaction in these terms as well. He may be expressing a deep-seated dissatisfaction the nature of which he is unaware, and yet when challenged can only represent it in the terms with which he is most familiar.

It is easy to understand the bewilderment of managers who complain, 'Our wages are better than others: our pensions are the most generous in industry: we emphasize the importance we place on security: we try to give the best working conditions, etc., and yet no one seems willing to do more than the minimum and some even try to hold back productivity. What more can we do?'

The 'more' that can be done falls into two phases. First, the recognition that malpractices of any kind are symptoms of many sorts of needs and are not merely physiological. Secondly, and most difficult of all, having acknowledged that appearances may be misleading, to try and identify the root causes of dissatis-faction.

As we have seen, when the lower physiological needs have been satisfied, they are no longer important. For practical purposes, they no longer exist. But at this point, the social needs become paramount—such needs as those for belonging and for accep-tance and the desire to be part of a recognizable and homo-geneous group. This is a perfectly natural phenomenon which reflects the natural gregariousness of people, particularly of manually employed people. It is for this reason that workers tend to come together in groups, in teams, in branches, in gangs, and that when these groupings grow too large, they tend to subdivide so that any individual develops a loyalty to the sub-group that often exceeds his attachment to the original aggregation.

Management, of course, has been aware of this tendency, but has generally reacted to it in a hostile fashion in the belief that it posed a threat to rational organization, and they have tried to thwart the practice. Other managers have endeavoured to oppose the proliferation of small groups with the notion of loyalty to the larger—i.e. the company. This is more intelligent and well-meaning, but it is a mistake to think that such loyalties are exclusive of others and more important. Personal loyalties proceed upwards from the smaller to the larger, but such is the irrationality of man that he will generally cling to the smaller whenever the possibility of conflict between the two becomes apparent. Thus, the gang in which a man is usually employed is more important to him than his trade union branch. His branch receives a greater measure of his support than his trade union. And, equally, his own union means more to him than the entire trade union movement. But he will defend even that movement when it is attacked by the State of which it is a part.

Thus, the phenomenon of 'groupness' is a fact of life and therefore of industry and, indeed, many studies have shown the tightly built working group can be more effective under proper conditions than the same number of separate individuals. Yet many managements have gone to considerable lengths to organize work in such a way as to break up these natural group-ings, and have been surprised that employees have become resistant and unco-operative.

Beyond the social needs exist a further level of satisfactions that, in a sense, emphasize again the individuality of man rather than his social side. These are the needs that relate to his self-esteem and to his reputation. They are needs that are of the greatest significance for it is in this area that the pursuit of satisfaction brings the greatest achievements for mankind. It is for this reason that it is right to think of an ascending order of satisfaction from the physiological; to safety; to social and to egotistical needs. The first and lower level of needs—for food, clothing and shelter—produce no motivation once these needs have been satisfied. But at the other end of the scale, these higher needs are rarely satisfied and man seeks indefinitely for more and more satisfaction once these needs have become important to him although they are not usually 'activated' until after the physiological, safety and social needs have been met. Thus, the needs for self-respect and self-confidence; for knowledge and achievement; for status and recognition; for respect and self-fulfilment, usually remain dormant until the lower level needs are satisfied. Thus the tragedy of modern industry is that too many employees actually need to concentrate on the lower level needs, while a great many more mistakenly believe that they have to continue to satisfy those needs, while egotistic needs lie below the level of their awareness.

It is surely, then, in this area of action that the greatest hope lies for a 'take-off' into a real 'age of affluence' that will rest on more secure foundations than at present. But it will do more than that, for the raising of a nation's productivity is not an end in itself. The extent to which we can achieve the raising of our material welfare, through the fulfilment of man's natural and legitimate satisfactions at the higher levels, will influence the extent to which we have moved from the Affluent Society to the Good Society.

CHAPTER VIII

THE PROBLEM OF CHANGE

THE last chapter but one threw into relief one of the deep-seated attitudes of workers towards management, even when they are not being prompted by experienced leaders of an organization that has weathered many industrial storms. They know that if management decides to introduce something new that they may be able to delay innovation, but they cannot stop it. While the procedure of introduction is being obeyed to the letter, with union officials and management representatives round the table, the innovation (sometimes in the guise of a 'pilot scheme') will have arrived. If, later on, union representatives succeed in finding appropriate means of making the change acceptable, all should be well. If not, a dispute is bound to follow. The lesson of this general conclusion is that innovation should be preceded by consultation, not accompanied by it.

We all tend to resist change, unless we know for certain that it is to our advantage. Two American industrial psychologists have made use of the Greek compound homeostasis to describe the principle of stability or constancy, the state in which most human beings prefer to exist. No one, in ordinary everyday life, chooses economic uncertainty, especially if he has family responsibilities that he takes seriously. Therefore, argue these psychologists, the reason 'for the formation of labor unions is that workers perceive such organizations as devices for preserving their homeostatic stability'.[1]

In other words, and simpler language, workers see in organized labour a counter to the employers' power to make unexpected changes in their circumstances. Thus, as Stagner and Rosen go on to point out, and as we have already seen, there

[1] Stagner and Rosen, *The Psychology of Union-Management Relations*, 1965, p. 128.

is an inherent conflict in the industrial situation. When the employers and managers have unrestricted control over working conditions the workers are powerless. When the workers encroach upon this power, the employer resists, because he fears that his control may be seriously diminished. Resistance to change, therefore, is not all one way. And a reasonably settled bargain need not be disadvantageous to one side or the other. There can often be gains for both sides. But if it is the power of decision and action that is being considered, any advance by one side must be seen as a retreat by the other. It does not necessarily follow, however, that labour is insatiable, as Stagner and Rosen seem to argue. They contend that union officers, having obtained all the concessions that their members have demanded, face 'the dilemma of success'. Having helped industrial workers to achieve satisfactory working conditions, they must still hunt around for more bones of contention in order to keep their members' support.

If that were true, innovation could provide a continuing series of pretexts around which to construct bargaining situations, which can help to give the union 'a reason for continued existence, [which] will protect us in our comfortable leadership posts'.[1] But this is surely a superficial conclusion compared with the less sophisticated and palpably more natural reaction of individuals, or groups, to the threat of unsettling change, which is to prefer the familiar to the less familiar, the known to the unknown. Discussing resistance to change in a textile mill, Fensham and Hooper comment that it can be taken to indicate 'that new relationships are not being successfully achieved or, rather, that they are not leading to improved satisfaction. Individuals and groups in a factory seek their own interests in the form of wages, enhanced respect, better working conditions, greater job satisfaction, and in many other ways. If 'resistance' can be seen as a positive seeking after these self-interests rather than a negative blocking of progress, the management of innovation will be simpler.'[2] The unsatisfactory relationships referred to here will arise from an absence of mutual confidence, a distrust of the management by the workers and vice versa, which may well be counterbalanced by a feeling on the part of the managers (whose attitude to work is

[1] *Op. cit.*, p. 129.
[2] *The Dynamics of a Changing Technology*, 1964, pp. 222–3.

substantially different) that petty self-interest is impeding the path of the company's progress.

As Burns and Stalker have suggested, resistance to change is not confined to the wage earners. The salary earners, even managing directors, can become involved when 'the actual and manifest changes which occur are seen as threats to the existing structure of power and status'. They reason that to resist adapting an organization or simply one's own position at work to the demands of rapid change 'is a measure of self-defence, which is a "natural" reaction'. Indeed, they point out that the ostensible purpose in the resisting action of people and groups may conceal other fears based on other motives, occupational, social or domestic. It seems reasonable to conclude that some individuals will take part in the resistance activity of a group because it blends in with some such inner motive of their own.

The way to tackle this complexity of feelings, suggest Burns and Stalker, is to create institutions within the firm, or so to alter the balance of existing institutions, that the needs thrown up by the changes will be taken into account. But, of course, the great difficulty lies in discovering what these needs really are, for they often turn out to be more complex than would generally be supposed by someone unfamiliar with the evolution of 'informal' relationships in industry. It would be unwise to assume that the higher ranks in factory, warehouse or office respond in a more complicated way to unexpected change, although in many cases they may have more to lose (or what amounts to the same thing in practice, they may believe that they have). But the closer one gets to the shop floor the more 'resistance to change' becomes related to job security, pay and conditions and less to status. So, while experience and the findings of social and psychological researchers support the view that to resist change is natural and common to all ranks in business, it is probable that, generally speaking, it is less 'pathological' among the shop-floor workers. Burns and Stalker use the word 'pathological' where resistance to change is offered even where technical progress at an increased rate may be regarded as necessary, desirable or healthy.[1]

In a study of technical and social interaction in a large steelworks, a team from Liverpool University drew the interesting conclusion that 'General attitudes, or predispositions, towards

[1] *The Management of Innovation*, 1961, p. 235 *et seq.*

technical change seem to be clearly related to occupational structure. The degree of approval of technical change declines as one descends the occupational hierarchy; the higher the status of a group, and the greater its interest in the present organisation of production, the more positive is its attitude.' They went on to distinguish between staff, maintenance and production workers, finding that 'maintenance workers show a more positive attitude towards technical change than production workers at the corresponding level', perhaps because maintenance men are craftsmen and have a more firmly rooted belief in the benefits of technical progress.[1]

Production workers, on the other hand, especially in the setting of steelworks as studied by this team, being less skilled and more committed in their training and experience to the existing nature of the production process, tend to be suspicious and therefore hostile to dangerous-seeming innovations. Nevertheless, the process workers in the steelworks investigated by the Liverpool University team showed a loyalty to the firm and an acceptance of the inevitability of a certain amount of redundancy in their working lives that seemed to counterbalance any hesitations about technical change. They did, however, pay attention to the effect of such change on their existing earnings, as compared with white-collar workers in the same firm, who worried more about promotion and opportunities for promotion.

There is an excellent recent example drawn from the steel industry of a well-handled technical innovation. In the United Steel Companies group it was known as the SPEAR project, the initials standing for Steel, Peech Electronic Arc Reorganization. This change involved, over the years 1962–64, the replacement of a large number of open hearth furnaces, tended by teams of melters, by half a dozen electronic arc furnaces requiring fewer melters with a different order of skill. Altogether about a thousand men were redeployed as a consequence of the new installations, and very few of them were made redundant. Some were found jobs in other parts of the United Steel group, and some were successfully retrained to operate the much larger and more productive units. Among the melters who were retrained there were men in their fifties, and at least one over

[1] Banks, Halsey, Lupton and Scott, *Technical Change and Industrial Relations*, p. 251 *et seq.*

sixty. This was regarded, with justification, as something of a triumph for the Steel, Peech and Tozer management, who went to a great deal of trouble, not only to ensure that as few men as possible suffered from the change, but to keep the whole labour force fully informed, so that they did not, at any stage, have to depend on outside sources of information (or rumour), such as the local newspapers, for knowledge of what was going on inside the place where they worked.

One of the obstacles with which the management had to contend in re-organizing the furnace teams was the tradition that a first-hand melter, when moved to another team, had to begin again at the bottom. The important thing was that they were aware of the customs of the trade and took them into account, but more than that, they also contrived to secure agreement from the union that to operate the new furnaces it was necessary that the melters should pass an examination for the City and Guilds certificate in electric arc steelmaking.

It would be unrealistic to conclude from this convincing example of the management of innovation that everybody involved was satisfied. It is impossible to be certain that every individual is happy about changes that affect him and his job in fundamental ways. But to be able to secure agreement and co-operation from the majority, inadequate though it may seem to those who have the individual's interests at heart, is a step in the right direction. As students of these situations recognize, as do experienced managers, a measure of compromise is inevitable. As the Liverpool University team concluded in their own investigation, 'management and workers are . . . dependent on each other; this must influence their readiness to compromise, as, for example, in the acceptance by the workers of management's right to effect changes provided that good conditions of employment and the seniority system were maintained'. Most workers can be persuaded to accept the necessity for technical progress once they come to realize that the survival of the company, and therefore of their jobs, depends on it, and furthermore that they stand eventually to gain material advantages from it. Although the immediate survival of Steel, Peech and Tozer and of the United Steel Companies group was not dependent upon the SPEAR project's success, the eventual competitive strength of the company and of the group was decisively affected. Certainly there were material gains

F

for many of the men involved, though not for all. Rarely in real life can all the ideal conditions that theory might demand be met with or created. The crucial aspect for management is to come as close to the idea as practical conditions will permit, and to be seen to be trying to achieve it. (A short description of the SPEAR project appears in Appendix 2).

Obviously one of the key conditions in securing the acceptance of change of job is security for the individual, both as an ethical consideration and as part of the necessary preliminaries to any introduction of change, technical or otherwise. There are at least two angles to job security in these circumstances, for in addition to the simple issue of ensuring that the individual remains in gainful employment, there is the more complex matter of job satisfaction. Many of the restrictive demarcation rules that have evolved over the years have the sole object of protecting one skilled occupation from encroachment by another, and therefore from eventual replacement either permanently or in the event of strikes. As Flanders says: 'Among the crafts this is potentially one of the most dangerous areas of conflict because of its impact on efficiency, its associations with job and union security and, not least, the inter-union character of the disputes it throws up'.[1]

Anyone who reads a daily newspaper knows that British industry has been bedevilled by demarcation disputes in increasing numbers and seriousness since the war, and a moment's thought suggests that the chief reason for craft union clashes must be the changing nature of technology. The crafts involved were for the most part developed as special skills more than a century ago, and some of them, like woodworking, are as old as the human race. A few, like electrical engineering, are much younger and often require an ability in their practitioners to use tools and techniques that appertain to other trades. If the incidental use of certain tools and materials brings one craft into collision with another either it can lead to loss of time in disputes or, on settlement, it can and often does lead to tedious and almost equally time-wasting patterns of work. This was certainly true at the Fawley refinery, where the records showed that there had been many demarcation disputes in the past. They had usually been settled on the part of the workers by the shop stewards. Nevertheless, 'Their main cost, and that

[1] *Op. cit.*, p. 46.

quite heavy, had been the expenditure of management's time in dealing with them'.[1]

In many industries the defensiveness of craft unions has proved to be an almost insuperable obstacle to technical improvement, in spite of the individual craftsman's readiness to see the necessity for it. Sometimes the conditions that employers have been obliged to observe on the introduction of new equipment has driven costs up rather than down in the long run, putting the firm's competitive position in jeopardy. In the printing industry there have been notable instances of resistance to innovation. Writing of the ever-widening technical possibilities in printing processes today (including automatic control, computer setting and photographic setting), Alan Delafons, a typographer and editor, said: 'All these changes will, of course, be fiercely resisted by the trade unions, loth to see the ever-ripening plums of higher pay for fewer hours (and less output) withered by the chill wind of technical development'. And, he adds, apart from the master printers themselves being slow to write off their old machinery and install new, 'They will also shrink from a possibly long and certainly costly war with the unions'. He points out that the hand compositors of the nineteenth century opposed the introduction of composing machines with tremendous bitterness, 'and the same attitude of mind has prevented or long retarded the introduction of new methods and new machines in the printing works in the second half of this twentieth century'.[2]

This is a familiar phenomenon in British industry as in most advancing industrial societies and has been described as a fear of change, rather than a simple objection to it or resentment of it. A consultant, who specialized during his lifetime in profit-sharing agreements as a possible solution to the problem of innovation and its impact on organized labour, has recorded his view that the fear of change on the part of workpeople has tended to be reinforced by the reluctance of company managements to re-examine their methods of payment to bring them into line with changed conditions of work. Unless the top management of a company realizes that adjustments in pay are a key constituent of any programme of productivity improvement they are unlikely to make much progress. 'The

[1] *Op. cit.*, pp. 46–7.
[2] *The Structure of the Printing Industry*, 1965, pp. 118–19.

leadership of any company depends entirely on the attitude of mind at directorial and executive level. A negative attitude at that level will induce the same attitude right through the company, whereas a positive one, which is always prepared to examine new methods and new approaches to any problem, will gradually build up that type of mind among all the staff and employees'.[1]

While this may be rather an optimistic statement, the writer, an experienced consultant, rightly judged that it makes little sense for managements to complain about difficult attitudes of mind on the shop floor if similar attitudes of mind are evidently prevalent in the boardroom. He was equally correct in pointing out that, in general, men are by nature co-operative, and therefore the cash solution is not of itself certain. 'You can secure your employees' attendance, you can secure their presence at a machine, you can even secure some output from them and the machine, but can you obtain their wholehearted assistance and co-operation in the business of the company by attempting to buy them? The answer has always proved to be in the negative.'[2]

F. R. Bentley was a strong advocate of what he called 'share of production' plans, as opposed to simple profit sharing which originated in the last century and was officially defined at the International Congress of Profit Sharing in Paris in 1889. Briefly, profit sharing is an agreement between employer and workers that the latter shall receive, in addition to their wages, a predetermined percentage of the company's profits. Naturally the profit margin on which this percentage will be levied depends on the success of the company in its trading, but it also depends on its accounting. From time to time the form of taxation on company profits has varied and this has affected the profit figure finally arrived at by the company. There have been times, too, when trading conditions have been so bad that many firms have found it difficult to produce a profit at all. After running a profit-sharing scheme for some years, to cease distributing an annual sum of money in addition to weekly pay packets causes protests from employees that their incomes have fallen. Finally, if workers are poorly paid, to distribute so-called profit shares looks too much like an empty attempt to

[1] F. R. Bentley, *People, Productivity and Progress*, 1964, pp. 105–6.
[2] *Op. cit.*, p. 107.

capture goodwill on the cheap. The popularity of profit-sharing schemes has accordingly fluctuated over the years, but generally speaking it can be said that they have never really caught on in most of British industry. A dedicated group of companies continues to operate them in a variety of ways, and some claim that they do succeed in winning co-operation from employees, who are thus able to realize that their prosperity is directly linked with the company's and therefore to the amount of productive effort they put into their work.

It is instructive to compare the motives behind the introduction of profit sharing and the reaction of trade unions to them. It is doubtful if employers regarded profit sharing as a means of reducing resistance to change. More likely, in the nineteenth century anyway, some of them felt that it was their moral duty to share the profits of their enterprise with their workpeople. Others no doubt hoped that by giving workers a small share in the equity of the company (the profits were often shared out in the form of stock, usually not transferable) they would be creating a palpable link between self-interest and company welfare, employees might then come to feel that the company was 'theirs' and would therefore cease restrictive practices, strikes and other unco-operative activity. Other, baser motives have been attributed to employers and managements in the introduction of profit sharing, such as desiring to keep wage rates stable by transferring fluctuations to the profit-sharing bonus.

However this may be (and the fact must be faced that profit-sharing has engendered some cynicism among rank-and-file workers) the trade unions have seldom felt very enthusiastic about it. Their view, apart from finding that profit-sharing tended to undermine their collective bargaining position, is that this is an attempt by employers to win their workers away from organized and militant labour (and some employers have made no secret of this ambition in the past). They also subscribe to the opinion that the true financial position of some companies is cleverly concealed, making it impossible for the worker to know if his share in the profits is realistic. On top of this charge, unionists point out that profitability depends more on competent management than on the performance of workers, whose efficiency derives for the most part from the quality of their equipment and materials. In short, profit sharing, as such, has failed to find universal favour in British industry, and seems unlikely ever to do so. Many writers add that, even where the scheme can be seen to be a genuine share out of genuine profits, it is still no royal road to better industrial relations. These have to be achieved independently of profit sharing or financial incentives.[1]

Bentley, an accountant by training, has pointed out that one of the chief weaknesses of profit sharing is the long intervals between 'hand-outs' and their consequent lack of connection with the job. 'Operatives invariably appreciate the additional cash but fail to understand when the annual payment is lower than that of the previous year'.[2] In the United States there has accordingly been a drift away from individual incentives and bonuses towards schemes more bound up with the company's general productivity. The Scanlon Plan, which varied from company to company in detail, was one such scheme, based on the relationship of wages to sales. The Rucker Plan, geared to sales value, was another, and Bentley himself introduced a version of it into a number of British firms.[3] The Bentley variant depended on an inspection of the company accounts over a period of past years in order to determine the ratio of costs to net earnings. On this basis Bentley would calculate what he termed the share of production value attributable to labour and which, he claimed, was invariable whatever economic conditions might prevail. An elementary account appears in his book, *People, Productivity and Progress*, and the merits of this particular productivity incentive scheme have been hotly debated. The point about Bentley's schemes to remember, however, is that they were aimed at demonstrating to employees in a material form the benefits to be gained from them by co-operating with management in making their company more efficient. Provided that this was understood there would obviously be far less resistance to innovation. But in spite of his plan's obvious advances over simple profit sharing, when Bentley died recently only a handful of firms in Britain had attempted to apply it.

There remains considerable doubt about the efficacy of

[1] A. B. Badger, *Man in Employment*, 2nd ed., 1966, chapter 32.
[2] *Op. cit.*, p. 60.
[3] An account of some of these schemes and their application appears in Appendix III.

financial incentives as a means of overcoming resistance to change, although common sense supports the belief that economic improvement is bound to help in the introduction of changes designed to render a company more profitable. Managements are sometimes inclined to feel that workers in highly mechanized plants tend to do rather too well at each stage of mechanical development. Their jobs are made easier and more productive without much if any extra effort being demanded from them, and they expect to be paid more, and usually more in proportion to the firm's increased profitability. Yet, runs the argument, they are taking none of the risk of investing in these innovations, and the management and the company's directors and shareholders are. It seems to be one of the facts of industrial life that workers and managers see their jobs and rewards from completely different angles.

No discussion of this vexed problem of incompatible objectives could be complete without reference to one of the most detailed studies yet made of the effects of change on all grades of employee in a company. Professor Elliott Jaques' *Changing Culture of a Factory* was first published in 1951. One of the changes he describes involved taking the service department, meaning the maintenance gangs, off piece-work payment, because it was inappropriate to their kind of work, and putting them on hourly rates. The enlightened management at the Glacier Metal Company allowed free and open discussion about the method and the scale of payment between workers' representatives, supervisors and senior managers. But, 'In the negotiations in the Service Department on the change-over in methods of payment, the early attempts of the management and of the workers' representatives to keep discussion narrowly focused solely on the wages question came to naught. Each time they tried so to confine themselves and to 'stick to the agenda', other issues crept in, causing intense frustration to everyone and creating the feeling that they were never to get anywhere. Eventually it became apparent that these so-called side-issues were not so unrelated to the problem at hand as at first they seemed. They contained in fact problems of relationship which had to be tackled *before the wages question could be successfully approached*.'[1]

Jaques does not put that last phrase in italics, but it contains

[1] P. 308.

the essence of the industrial sociological problem. Contrary to common belief, the money question is not the whole, but only a part, though an important and a vital part. A factor that must be counted in nowadays is, of course, full employment, patchy though it may be in terms of regions and industrial areas, and industries. Another is the institution of political democracy, which extends to every adult citizen, no matter how humble or how poor, a say in the final decision as to who shall govern. Given these two rights, the right to work and the right to vote in secret for the party of his choice, it should not surprise us that this same citizen feels, even subconsciously, that he also ought to have some right to be consulted about the future of 'his' job and 'his' company. In the confrontation at Glacier, which took place quite soon after the war, management and workers indulged in what Jaques has described as a 'severe mutual test-out'.

'Management took every opportunity of allowing the workers to demonstrate how responsibly they were capable of behaving. The workers did not miss a single occasion to test whether the management really intended to be as co-operative and as above-board as they professed. The fundamental issue was whether relations based on mutual confidence could be established. . . .' And is not this the fundamental issue itself?

CHAPTER IX

FALSE REMEDIES

PROFESSOR ELTON MAYO, one of the pioneers of the human relations movement in industry, said in his book, *The Social Problems of an Industrial Civilization*, that one of the illusions among engineers, economists and university people is that morale, 'the maintenance of co-operative living, is commonly spoken of as an imponderable, an intangible . . .'. He added, 'The fact is that those who refer to such matters as imponderable are themselves ignorant of the methods by which they can systematically set about the task of improving the co-operative morale in a working department, and are irked by any implication that this is the proper duty of the administrator. Such men therefore rely upon a confident, or even jolly, manner, upon knowing everyone's first name and using it, upon expedients such as saying "Good morning" to everyone they meet. And it is these same persons who express contempt for "sentimental" methods'.[1]

Such, unfortunately, is still the widely held view of what human relations in industry is all about. It is a superficial view, to say the least, and, as Elton Mayo remarked twenty years ago, would be comic in an isolated instance, but as a substitute for intelligent inquiry gathers about it an element of tragedy. 'It is a short step from friendship or tolerance to distrust and hatred when the normal relationships disintegrate.' If the relationships between different grades or classes of people in industry have no stronger foundation than temporary amiability when all is going well within the firm, the likelihood is that goodwill can be discounted almost entirely in times of stress and conflict.

A great many attempts have been made to comprehend the nature of the relationships that arise between men at work. In the eyes of those persons who, frustrated by apparently irrational clashes of interests, have mentally regressed to a nostalgic and uncritical position, the present situation in industry

[1] 1945, pp. 118-19.

is unnecessarily complex, whereas 'in the good old days you knew where you stood'. In short, the simpler, cruder master-and-man relationship with its phenomena of relentless hire and fire, casual labour, class hatred and eventual technical backwardness acquires, in the mind of the frustrated man, even when he is moderately intelligent and well informed, an attractiveness that seduces him into attitudes and utterances that can only render the prevailing situations worse. As J. A. C. Brown comments, 'In industry, the main symptoms of regression are lack of emotional control, responsiveness to rumours, inadequate social organization, and blind loyalties for certain people or organizations. . . . On the side of management, hypersensitivity, refusal to delegate authority, inability to distinguish between reasonable and unreasonable requests, and stupid generalizations on the subject of labour or political questions, may also be evidence of regression'.[1]

Looking at British industry since the war, which is now more than twenty years away, one can discern on the part of management a search for solutions, first to the problems of worker behaviour—absenteeism, labour turnover, 'systematic soldiering', accidents, waste and scrap, bad timekeeping, uncooperativeness—and secondly to the problem of bad industrial relations, especially unofficial actions on the part of shop stewards and *ad hoc* works committees. So far, there seems to have been very little success to record, although the catalogue of remedies is long and many self-styled experts have enriched themselves by providing them to industrial companies in the form of consultancy. A marginal but not untypical example of the kind of offer with which usually shrewd businessmen and managers have been confronted is the poster service. Several agencies, some of them American, established themselves in Britain ten or twelve years ago, charging remarkably high fees for a fortnightly or monthly poster service. These posters, many of them extremely well designed and printed, would be sent to the company's personnel department or to the managing director of a firm too small to sustain even one personnel officer, with the object of displaying them in prominent places about the factory site and perhaps the offices. They would propagate such matters as safety, punctuality, cost consciousness, even 'togetherness' in the best evangelical manner.

[1] *The Social Psychology of Industry*, 1954, p. 253.

The poster, of course, is no more than one small and not specially powerful weapon in the general campaign to capture the attention and potentially the goodwill of the worker. As Michael Ivens suggests in his comprehensive text on 'communication'[1] (a fashionable term at one time and almost always pronounced misleadingly with a final 's'), posters designed by the workpeople themselves look more convincing than slick agency series that are better designed and worded but look as if they had been produced by clever outsiders. Some of the welfare organizations like the Industrial Society and the Royal Society for the Prevention of Accidents sell posters, the former on suggestion schemes, the latter on safety. The first kind produce tangible, if not impressive results. The effect of the second is harder to measure. As to general 'goodwill' campaigns, one would suspect that they do most good for the supplier. Certainly, for managers to hope that posters or any other isolated communication 'ploy' (like pay packet slips, house magazines, notice boards, works outings and other social events) will do their job of establishing sound worker-management relations for them would suggest that they have no real notion of how to set about it in the first place.

This book has attempted to indicate, in its early chapters, how the two sides of industry have emerged and how their attitudes to one another have developed as industry has become more and more dominant in our lives. What many people have failed to grasp is that social progress outside a company has sometimes been more rapid and beneficial than inside, although in some isolated instances a few companies have led the way. But in the last fifty years we have entered and are now leaving a phase of revolutionary change in our national institutions. Time was when the upper and middle classes always knew best—or assumed they did. (Beatrice Webb herself remarked on this in her diary: 'There is no such thing as spontaneous public opinion; it all has to be manufactured from a centre of conviction and energy radiating through persons . . .'. She remarked on another occasion what a good thing it was that she and her friends were the right kind of persons.)[2] And among the tangle of motives with which social historians have struggled one could discern enlightened self-interest coupled with the sort of calculated

---

[1] *The Practice of Industrial Communication*, 1963, pp. 184–6.
[2] *Our Partnership*, 1948, pp. 259–60.

altruism that led H. G. Wells to call Sidney Webb *The New Machiavelli*.

The problem of modern Britain, however, remains that we have a democratic political framework (or ostensibly so) within which there still function a variety of undemocratic institutions. Companies, as the law stands at present, must rank as undemocratic in the extreme, for the votes that control them go to money and not to people. That is to say that, nominally at least, the shareholders run the company and therefore the people in it, while in practice the running is done by a small and powerful group called the Board of Directors, few of whom are usually working managers, and whose right to take part in the high level decision-making of their company resides in the quantity of shares they hold or the fact that they have been selected by the rest of their colleagues on the board.

'The directors of British companies are a small élite; about 30,000, it was estimated in the 'fifties, for all public companies together,' says Michael Fogarty. There are also the directors and partners in private concerns and they are, for the most part, drawn from similar class backgrounds (over a third of the managers in large companies were graduates when a count was taken thirty years ago). Even those directors who are not upper or middle class in origin (like democracy, these are commonly used but not clearly defined terms) tend, if they prosper, to acquire the appurtenances and tastes of the level of society to which they have aspired.

Add to these broadly acceptable facts that 'British company law still formally requires directors to act in the interests of shareholders alone, or rather to consider the interests of employees, customers, or the country only in so far as this may also advance the shareholders' interests', and it becomes clear that the division of interests that some well-meaning observers of industry had thought non-existent in modern society still persists. What is more, and more important to the understanding of labour relations, it is also manifest to the employees that this state of affairs exists, and that they (although they would seldom be able to cite law on the matter) rank below the shareholders as a managerial preoccupation.[1]

---

[1] Cf. Michael Fogarty, *Company and Corporation—one Law?*, 1965. The quotations are from p. 1 and p. 7.

There were attempts in the early 1950s to educate employees in the intricacies of company finance, so that they might understand better what share of the gross revenue of a company was spent upon raw materials, overhead costs, wages and salaries, what proportion remained as profit before tax, and what small share of the net profit was then distributed to the shareholders in dividends. In 1954 the British Institute of Management published a lengthy text called *Presenting Financial Information to Employees*, which indicated various methods of conveying simple facts about money via the house magazine or some other printed medium to the simple-minded lads and lasses on the shop floor. Several companies made, and still make, valiant efforts to be frank and fearless in this way. One company chairman, Mr Weston Howard of Hayward-Tyler, even went as far as to say, when questioned on the point, that he would willingly reveal his own salary and directors' fees to his employees, should they ask. Apart from the remoteness of the possibility that any of them, other than someone of aggressive temperament, would do such a thing, Mr Howard found himself virtually alone in taking frankness this far. It could be argued that he was wrong for, were his income as high as, say, Lord Beeching's or Sir William Lyons', it could have had the opposite effect from the one intended.

As we have already noted, money is not the whole of the question, but it lies at the heart of it. The trade unions have for years taken the trouble to acquire ordinary shares in the companies for which their members work so that they may see the annual accounts and attend the Annual General Meeting. But the sophisticated among them know that a balance sheet tells only part of the story, and that accounting practice enables companies to own valuable assets whose book value, as displayed in the accounts, may be a fraction of real worth, as well as that the categories under which income and expenditure are listed in the published accounts can conceal many benefits for shareholders. In brief, suspicion and mistrust, which have dogged labour relations for years, are not as easily allayed by a dazzling display of bar charts and pie diagrams, or beautifully sketched heaps of coins, as some would-be enlightened executives have at times supposed.

This is not to say that the bare rules of 'communication', which may be boiled down to prompt accurate, understandable and unequivocal two-way information, have no value. Naturally they have. Thousands of words have poured out on the subject of clarity of expression, both in the written and spoken word. Public speaking, committee control and procedure, report writing, negotiation, the entire gamut of making contact through language has been worked over as a rich field for management experts. But seldom, if ever, is emphasis given to the much more vital matter of unspoken mutual confidence. Misunderstanding is often the product of hostility, a preconceived expectation that distorts meaning. There was an instance of this kind in an award by the Industrial Court of an additional 2d an hour to a group of workers in a small London factory whose union had applied for arbitration. The men thought that they would receive an extra 6s 8d a week, and came out on strike when they did not. The employers, who were inclined to assume that the Industrial Court was on their side, had not read the award as meaning an additional 2d an hour on the basic wage. All the men in the factory being on bonus payments as well as overtime, the board had interpreted the award to mean that they did not need to pay any more. Attitudes therefore have a strong influence on interpretation, and it is the attitudes towards which the managerial effort should be directed. Playing with words may have some effect, but it cannot be as fundamental as honest dealing by both sides. Unfortunately, like Elton Mayo's hail-fellow-well-met manager, who hopes to carry the day with a smile and a big hello, there are also managers who have developed an extraordinarily subtle way of saying nothing while meaning something, and saying something while meaning nothing. This is a fine political skill, that may have a place in business dealing, but harmful rather than helpful where the atmosphere is already highly charged in the negative polarity. 'Actions', as the proverb has it, 'speak louder than words.' It is more important to act with discretion and thoughtfulness than to make speeches or publish statements, especially if the two do not appear to match. One could add, at the risk of cluttering the argument with clichés, that justice needs to be seen to be done, as well as done. But what is justice, in this industrial setting, and who shall say when it has been done?

There is, then, an important basic task for management which cannot be accomplished by recourse to palliatives or superficial remedies in bringing about stable and constructive labour relationships: the implanting in all levels of employees of the belief, the genuine belief, that the management plays fair. Surprisingly, that message can be transmitted without having to be splashed in bold type in the company newspaper or read out in basic English over closed-circuit television. It arrives unheralded but as certainly as any homing pigeon in the behaviour and treatment of his subordinates by every manager and supervisor in the company on each and every working day. There is always the unstable individual in every organization, but they do not do much harm and their activity can be well contained in a stable and confident atmosphere.

Apart from the communication myth (which is only mythical in so far as it is supposed to achieve miracles on its own) there is the welfare myth. Bad working conditions, it has been argued, can be overlooked in an atmosphere of mutual trust and confidence and of worthwhile activity. There are libraries full of books full of examples of human courage and endurance in the face of impossible and dangerous circumstances. Even now, a quarter of a century afterwards, we hear on all sides wistful longings for a return of the 'Dunkirk spirit'. It might well return—at another Dunkirk! But, on the whole, it is not the man on the shop floor who sighs for Dunkirk but his boss, who has vague and sentimental memories of dutiful and courageous behaviour on the part of quite ordinary and unimpressive seeming private soldiers. If he set fire to his factory he might find out that he had a hero in overalls on the premises. More likely there would be a rush for the fire escape. It is misleading and foolish, therefore, to assume that a particular set of circumstances will automatically reproduce responses in people that arose in a similar situation but with a fundamental difference below the surface. At Dunkirk men helped other men who were in danger. In civilian life, in industry, we are driven by quite different and rather more selfish motives.

A desire to pander to the material aspects of human desires underlies the welfare movement in industry, even though it began as a matter of moral obligation on the part of enlightened employers. Before there were such privileges as lavatories on the works premises, washrooms (older readers may remember the battles for pithead baths for coalminers in the years when the collieries were small and privately owned), subsidized canteens, sports clubs (which never gained much support) and a dozen other 'physical amenities', including subsidized company housing, there was worker-proprietor mistrust. The welfare concessions have done little to allay this, and in some instances have had the opposite effect, and aroused the suspicions of organized labour. This can sometimes happen if the concessions are too obviously offered as 'sops to Cerberus', as an underhand means of influencing workpeople in favour of the company's policies, even though they have had no voice in them. It degenerates even further when welfare becomes merely a matter of attracting labour or loyalty as a substitute for more straightforward methods. This, again, is not to decry welfare, but to put it in its proper perspective. In modern Britain good working conditions, with adequate lighting, heating and ventilation, and all the facilities that would be provided in an up-to-date school building, should be taken for granted and not therefore proffered as favours. Any other view is sadly dated and can lead only to embittered labour relations.[1]

It might be added that the paternalistic approach to labour relations has no place in modern industry either. The old attitude that 'we have done a lot for them, and they should be grateful to us' will not do. It was basically misconceived, anyway, because once the worker became sophisticated in his attitude to work and his employer he was bound to question the taking away with one hand (or apparently underpaying) and giving back with the other, admitted by Lord Leverhulme (see Chapter II). And even if he did not or could not, his trade union took up the cry.

Paternalism, which remains with us yet, is a survival from the past. It cannot be called 'wrong', any more than any human institution or action done with good intent can. But it no longer has a place in modern industry and consequently has nothing to offer to the solution of our industrial problems.

There is another survival, however, that flourishes strongly, in spite of opposition, and that is the remarkably contrasted treatment that is meted out to hourly paid shop-floor workers, on the one hand, and to weekly or monthly paid office staff on the other. This is often argued about in terms of the old hand in the machine shop, with twenty years' service with the company, whose secretarial daughter is being paid twice his earn-

[1] Cf. Brown, *op. cit.*, pp. 280–1.

ings for a much pleasanter job. What really matters, however, is not the artificially high rate of pay for secretaries, which may be a temporary phenomenon, but that if the father were ill, he would not be paid, but that if his daughter were, she would. In fact, it is common, all over British industry, to treat the white-collar worker better than the man in overalls. The clerk, nowadays, objects to being paid less than the production-line man, but if earnings are compared it is frequently found that the man on the assembly line depends on bonuses and overtime, and therefore works a longer week for his money than the clerk.

The two systems of payment, whether the shop-floor worker is paid by piecework systems or by time, derive from the differing nature of the work. It is only quite recently that any attempt has been made to measure the output of office staff and to pay some of them by results, and such experiments have met with strong resistance. The cost of office work, like the cost of research and development, design, advertising and public relations, is not yet as measurable as the tangible products of the factory, about which is known all the essential information— the value of the raw materials, the time taken to work them up and so on. For the time being, then, it has to be accepted that methods of remuneration will differ, though some rationalization in the near future would be a step towards greater efficiency. But the different fringe benefits of staff and 'works' is an unnecessary and potentially embarrassing survival, and a handful of companies has been taking steps in recent years to abolish them as much as possible. Sickness payment schemes were among the first to be brought in by progressive employers, but wherever they did absenteeism through illness immediately increased, a disappointing and disillusioning occurrence. Dr J. A. C. Brown attributes this phenomenon to 'an atmosphere of dissatisfaction and poor morale', which cannot be overcome simply by offering free medical and dental attention, sick pay and even pension schemes, few of which were available to workpeople before the last war. One must not overlook the fact that, in certain industries and companies, employees who have become accustomed to job security and have ceased to fear the penalties of illness and old age, are inclined to look upon these benefits as rights,[1] while the individual employer, who has

[1] *Op. cit.*, pp. 280-1.

G

taken serious risks in establishing his enterprise in the first place, may, like his senior managers, recoil from such attitudes, there are at least two points to bear in mind in this connection. First, advanced industrial countries have for years been subject to political and religious pressures that have brought about a state of affairs in which the citizen has come to look upon himself as to some extent protected by the State from the cradle to the grave. This is the Welfare State idea. Secondly, and for various reasons that are not wholly relevant here, in spite of these advances in welfare and in standards of living, there remain obvious and not always comprehensible differences in the benefits derived from an enterprise by the élite that runs it as compared with the mass of workers who, as they might put it, get the work done.

The first will not have had the approval of all businessmen, even if they have never actively opposed the onset of 'gas and water Socialism'. The second comes, for many entrepreneurs and executives, under the heading of 'none of their business'. Unfortunately for good industrial relations, the workpeople and the trade unions have made it their business, and it has therefore to be taken into account, together with the cynicism that has not been dissipated over the years about the activities of the City of London, speculators, take-over bidders and financiers of all kinds, good and bad, large and small. In fact, in a company where mutual confidence exists, extreme generalizations about 'us' and 'them' are seldom heard. But even where they are, such thoughts and utterances should be regarded as symptoms, not causes, in any sense of the word. A busy and contented man rarely wastes his time in loose and ill-informed argument.

Under the surface of relationships at work, then, subsists a layer of opinion and prejudice about life, social class, rewards and penalties that is not easy to discount, although it may be all too easy to decry. It has become important to management in the past two decades because, with full employment and the Welfare State, the cruder take-it-or-leave-it manner towards labour can no longer work. It has become imperative to understand one another. Basically this is what the 'human relations movement' of a decade or so ago was all about, and why it commanded the support of the Ministry of Labour under Sir Walter Monckton (later Lord Monckton). It was doomed from the start, because by its very nature it was a superficial attempt to solve a profound problem.

The same benevolence lies behind the Marlow Declaration, signed by eminent men in all walks of life, including the trade unions, in January 1963, after a long weekend at the Compleat Angler, an expensive hostelry on the Thames at Marlow. The Marlow Foundation now tries, through research, education and propaganda of all kinds, to spread the gospel of goodwill in industry. It has been tried before (Mondism was an inter-war example, created under the stress of industrial discontent), but so far without lasting success. The differences between management and labour can only be properly and lastingly resolved at work, for it is at work that the individual encounters most of the elements that determine his attitude to life and society. His occupational importance—the regard that he receives as a result of his skills and experience, the enjoyment or otherwise of his work, the link with his workmates, and his income—are all determined at the workplace. To the extent that he is a cipher in the work system, doing a repetitive job at a pace set by machinery, looked down upon as unskilled or semi-skilled, paid by an incomprehensible system of piece-rates and set output norms by men in white coats, the more will he feel out of place and therefore indifferent to the demands of management.

If this same worker, or a number of them, enjoy more regard in their working group or in their local community (they will usually be highly thought of by their families), it is there that their loyalties will be fixed. This in itself puts the onus on management to bear in mind the individuality of people at work and not to behave, especially in times of change, as if they were all identical and therefore identically obedient and receptive. Appeals to do their best for the firm, for its customers, for exports and even for their country, are much more likely to make an impact if they come from directors and managers who have always shown an awareness of this sensitive relationship. Employers who recognised this state of affairs a long time ago tried various ways of taking shop-floor workers into the counsels of the company. Joint consultation, which is the subject of the next chapter, arose in this way.

CHAPTER X

JOINT CONSULTATION

'In the English-speaking world institutions which desire to maintain and improve their position must at all hazards bring themselves into line with democracy.' The words are from the 1906 edition of *Industrial Democracy* by Sidney and Beatrice Webb.[1] They were, oddly enough, directed at the trade unions of the time and not at business, for the Webbs felt that certain trade union practices were doomed to failure in a democratic State and ought to be surrendered in anticipation of their becoming outdated. They were particularly averse to 'the doctrine of vested interests', 'the device of restriction of numbers' and of the consequences of collective bargaining—'the fixing, by mutual agreement between the directors of industry and the manual workers, of special rates of wages for special classes'. The first we know as 'resistance to change', the second as 'restricting entry to a trade', and the third, about which the Webbs felt quite strongly, is the backbone of modern industrial relations.

The Webbs had not, of course, encountered our modern phenomenon of the unofficial strike. They did point to the widespread effects of strikes on sections of the community unconnected with the dispute, and decided that a democratic State would be compelled to intervene and enforce arbitration 'by an authoritative fiat. The growing impatience with industrial dislocation will, in fact, be where collective bargaining breaks down, and lead to its supersession by some form of compulsory arbitration; that is to say, by Legal Enactment. And when the fixing of the conditions on which any industry is to be carried on is thus taken out of the hands of the employers and workmen, the settlement will no longer depend exclusively on the strategic

[1] P. 809.

position of the parties, or of the industry, but will be largely influenced by the doctrine of a living wage'.[1]

This charge of being undemocratic was levelled at the unions because, by the time *Industrial Democracy* was published, they had begun to demonstrate their enormous bargaining strength. The title of this huge book, however, would have led some unionists to suppose that it argued the case of workers' representation in the control of companies, if not industries. Many unions, indeed, had written into their rules some general ambition to nationalize or otherwise obtain control of their industry, or at some early stage in their history passed a resolution akin to the one moved by the miners at the 1892 TUC. The wording insisted that the produce of the bowels of the earth must be national property and 'that the enterprise should also be, like the Post Office, a state department'.[2]

The literature of trade unionism and the working-class movement generally is full of demands for what was called by the Trades Union Congress and the Labour Party in a manifesto in 1924, *The Waste of Capitalism*, their 'passionate desire . . . for a greater share in determining the conditions under which the industrial machine works, for more responsibility, more recognition, more power, as an indispensable factor in production'. This desire, recorded the manifesto, was strongest in the younger generation of worker, who was no longer content with a state of affairs that 'makes him a slave. The status desired is that of a freeman.' Slavery took the form of being subordinated to the machine, which the writers saw as unavoidable, but capable of mitigation by shorter hours of work, better use of leisure and the distribution of the necessary drudgery of machine production 'as equally as possible, giving up all idea of having a privileged class which is freed from all distasteful duties'. Another aspect of industrial slavery was 'the subordination of the individual to the organization . . .'. They saw the enterprise as having developed a form of discipline that was basically military, reducing the worker to 'a mere cog in the machine, a pawn to be moved hither and thither by someone in authority who is carrying out a policy which the subordinate not only does not help to determine, but by the very nature and objects of which are kept hidden from him'.

[1] Webbs, *op. cit.*, pp. 813–15.
[2] R. Page Arnot, *The Miners*, 1949, p. 184.

Bearing in mind that this outspoken document is only forty years old, there must be men still at work who read and agreed with such statements. And who would deny the hard core of truth in much of it, while making allowances for the fashionably hyperbolic language? 'There he is, to his own seeming, a feeble unit in the midst of a huge organization which takes no account of him as a human being—he is merely one of the "hands"—helpless to affect his environment in the slightest degree. Is it any wonder the worker does not feel strongly impelled to wear himself out producing more and more profits for the employer? The wonder is that production continues at all. . . .'

The final sentence illustrates the point made by the Webbs. 'Autocracy is as out of date in industry as in civil government'.[1] It was not, even then, just a matter of nationalization, but of workers' participation in management that was in the minds of such writers. The late G. D. H. Cole pointed out in his *Introduction to Trade Unionism* that nationalization had come to be regarded as nothing more than State capitalism, and little better than private enterprise capitalism, without joint control by workers and management, 'both in relation to workshop management and the question of discipline'.[2] As far as trade union leaders and their members were concerned, therefore, the concept of industrial democracy embodied (and it took various forms from Robert Owen's idealistic labouring communities to syndicalism and guild socialism) workers' participation, so that when nationalization came after the Second World War trade union officers were appointed to the Boards of the public corporations which ran the industries and provision was made for forms of joint consultation at all levels, generally derived from the recommendations of the Whitley Committees (see Chapter IV). A full description of these arrangements has been given by Hugh Clegg in *Industrial Democracy and Nationalisation*,[3] where he points out that works committees have been compulsorily established and not left dependent upon the goodwill of employers.

The working of joint consultation in nationalized industry has, however, encountered some obstacles, outlined by Clegg, that are not unfamiliar in the private sector. 'Reasons for

[1] Milne-Bailey, *Trade Union Documents*, 1929, pp. 67–71.
[2] Cited in M. Beer, *A History of British Socialism*, 1948, p. 375.
[3] 1951, p. 67 *et seq.*

failure are not hard to find. Often the workers' representatives do not take readily to the work. The guild socialist belief that there was a sufficient number of workers able and eager to take part in running industry once the obstacles of capitalism were removed had no general validity. The workers' representatives understand the process of bargaining and are ready to use it to their advantage if they can, but in advisory committees "talking money" is debarred, and they are apt to think that this makes the committees of little importance. Their interest must then be aroused and fostered by the other side, for, except in so far as representatives of the technical staff are also present, the servicing of the committee depends on the management; only the manager can tell the committee of plans for the future and of the ways in which they are expected to affect the establishment; only the manager can authorize action on the committee's decisions. The manager, however, has no training, and may have no flair for this kind of work'.[1]

The same general lack of interest in joint committee work had dogged the Civil Service Whitley Councils in their early years, says Clegg, but as both sides got used to the work so the activity and effectiveness of the councils grew. At least both these groups of joint consultative committees began with the advantage that their members were drawn from the upper and lower ranks of public services and therefore the inevitable 'two sides' atmosphere encountered in private industry was considerably watered down. Nevertheless, such committees had to deal with matters of great importance to one side at least, notably redundancy, which would probably never have come before a joint committee in a company. Certainly the nationalized industries had to honour both the consultative procedure and the obligation confirmed by it, to provide substantial compensation to those who were dismissed. No such restrictions applied to private industry before the Redundancy Payments Act with the consequence that the approach to such situations varied widely from one company to another, just as the use of joint consultation varied.

One of the legacies of the post-war period has been a falling off in interest in what for the duration of the war had come to be known as joint production committees, when it was assumed that both management and workers had a common interest in

[1] *Op. cit.*, pp. 69-70.

getting together round a table to work out methods of stepping up output. It has even been claimed that one of the stimuli towards the establishment of works councils and committees, to give another pair of names, came from the more militant shop stewards.[1]

However that may have been, there could be little doubt that once the stimulus of war emergency had been removed the attention of both sides would shift on to matters more connected with conditions at work, grievances and domestic issues generally, with the one subject of prime importance generally barred from discussion. The fact that national agreements and similar high-level collective bargaining decisions were bound to take away from joint consultative committees any business to do with wages and earnings meant that they seemed secondary in importance. Even though some of the matters within the competence of joint committees could be of local importance, there would be a strong inclination to consider them inferior because of the absence of one overriding objective, wartime productivity or the peacetime pay packet.

It is also true that, in some companies, workpeople have tended to regard work councils as a management stunt, sometimes especially when the managing director himself takes the chair. One strong reason for this feeling on the part of the workers' side may be that this attempt to talk 'man to man', when everyone present knows that one group round that table has 'hire and fire' powers over the other, creates a highly artificial atmosphere (akin to the temporary and completely false ambience in the Army at Christmas when the officers and senior NCO's wait upon the private soldiers at dinner). Writers on this well-worn subject reiterate that joint consultation can never work unless both sides believe in it. Sometimes the blame has been laid at management's door for concentrating upon trivial matters of discussion and withholding from the agenda any subjects that might be held to interfere with 'management's right to manage', a fairly inclusive category. In short, the more reality that can be injected into what is essentially an artificial situation the more convinced and encouraged will the participants be, especially from the 'weaker' side. Where the managers who have to attend such committees are put in the position of confining the agenda to welfare questions, leaving all bigger

---

[1] Jenkins and Mortimer, *op. cit.*, p. 99.

issues to be referred back to senior management or to the Board, they will themselves feel hostile or at best indifferent to the proceedings, and in extreme cases will have constant recourse to that familiar evasion that the matter just raised is not within their terms of reference (even when it is).

When the National Institute of Industrial Psychology conducted its inquiry into joint consultation in 1948, sponsored by the Human Factors Panel of the Government Committee on Industrial Productivity, it came to the interesting and unequivocal conclusion that on the management side there was a feeling, especially marked at the senior levels, that joint consultation was a good thing because it gave them an opportunity to make their company a 'good social institution' where employees could be sure of a reasonable standard of living and at the same time 'satisfy their psychological needs'. Senior management, therefore, gave its blessing to the idea of joint consultation, but faith in its effectiveness and value tended to get weaker down the line. This tendency is reinforced in those companies where top management takes upon itself the task of sitting down with the workers' representatives, virtually excluding the middle and lower ranks of management from the system. The foremen are particularly ill served by such an arrangement, which is not as uncommon as might be supposed, because they feel the first effects upon the production line workers of management decisions that affect morale. The NIIP even encountered companies where the foremen were not represented as such on the works council, but voted with the men under them for a workers' representative. 'In such circumstances, lacking sufficient status, the foreman will not possess the necessary authority to exercise a proper leadership role and will tend therefore to become a mere mouthpiece for management. He may well feel, as was apparent in some firms, that the foreman is given all the unpleasant matters to convey and none of the pleasant ones in the communication between management and workers.'[1] Some writers have even stated that the consultative committee system puts the workers' representatives in the position of knowing more 'of the plans and purposes of higher management' than the foremen, who have been described elsewhere as management's 'front line'.[2]

[1] *Joint Consultation in British Industry*, 1952, p. 236.
[2] Flanders and Clegg, *op. cit.*, p. 325.

Where the link between top management and the shop-floor representation is as strong as that, one or two levels of management are in danger of being squeezed out of the consultation procedure, and eventually the whole process may fall into disrepute by creating more confusion and conflict than it prevents. Here lies one of the causes for the lack of support for joint consultation that has been evident in British industry, the other main cause probably being the absence of any agreement on the purpose of works councils. As T. E. Chester and Hugh Clegg have noted in their chapter on joint consultation,[1] there are two views of the objects of consultative procedure, at either end of a spectrum of opinion. At one extreme, as we have noted earlier, there are those who regard consultation as a step on the way towards industrial democracy, when management and workers will jointly operate the enterprise, acting as business partners, in complete contrast to the image of collective bargaining, which is merely haggling between opponents for economic advantages. At the other extreme, where most employers and managers are to be found, consultation is looked upon as restricted to complaints, grievances and disciplinary matters; welfare and safety; and, with luck and goodwill on both sides, efficiency in the factory. The last may take the form of informing the men about time studies or rate setting, and, in some companies, even descend into bargaining about rates. Hare has listed a fourth category of subject that may come within the competence of a works council: 'commercial and financial problems, the purchase of materials, the sales of the product and the finance of the business', adding that the distinction between this group of subjects and the three listed above is difficult to draw. But he also admits that in practice the trivial matters, such as complaints, are the easiest to have on the agenda, while 'discussion of the organization of the human factor requires a greater amount of co-operation . . .'. To talk about the business side at all seriously, he goes on, would call for a 'high degree of co-operation and mutual trust'.[2]

It is useful to have this corroboration from an academic source, because the concept of joint consultation as a whittled-down version of the once popular dream of industrial democracy is now so remote in time and so out of gear with modern

---

[1] Flanders and Clegg, *op. cit.*, pp. 326–7.
[2] A. E. C. Hare, *The First Principles of Industrial Relations*, 1965, pp. 134–5.

trade union thought that, although the literature of socialism is full of it, it is hard to believe that anyone either holds or tries to pursue it any longer. Yet, in a rudimentary way, workpeople who take part in works councils begin with the feeling that they are going to help run the business. Management, on the other hand, generally starts from the viewpoint that the works council may do whatever it likes, so long as it does not try to run the business.

The failure of joint consultation to take a permanent hold on British industry has sometimes been ascribed to the absence of legal enforcement, such as exists in Germany under the *Mitbestimmungsrecht* or Co-determination Law of 1951 which revived the workers' councils that had been superseded by Nazi nominees and gave them legal support. This law obliges companies in the coal and iron and steel industries to set up supervisory boards of directors with five out of eleven members elected from among the labour force. The eleventh man is elected by the ten who represent the two sides, and the five workers' members are allowed to select one member of the main board of management, who is known as the Labour Director. The system has since spread to other industries in Germany and appears to have led to greatly improved industrial relations, though it has met with criticism from time to time. Indeed, there was a national crisis over the introduction of co-determination by law into other industries, and the compromise measure passed by the Federal Parliament under the then Chancellor Dr Adenauer reduced the competence of works councils over management matters. Nevertheless, the Deutsche Gewerkschaftsbund, the West German TUC, supports the present watered-down form of co-determination and, according to one observer, is perfectly happy at the priorities generally followed by German works council presidents: 'His first loyalties tend to be to his fellow-workers, his second to the management, and the union comes third, because many problems are ironed out without bringing in the union at all.'[1]

The history of German works councils goes back more than a century to the abortive proposal of the Constitutional Assembly in Frankfurt during 1848-49, to set up such Councils (Fabrikausschüssen). Then consultative councils were actually set up in the Prussian mines in 1905, after which the 1916 Auxiliary

[1] Jossleyn Hennessy, 'The German "Miracle"', in *Economic Miracles*, Institute of Economic Affairs, 1964, pp. 22-9.

Service required the appointment of workers' or employees' councils in all enterprises with fifty or more employees. This development was reinforced under the Weimar Constitution.

After the defeat of Hitler, under whom the councils were superseded by appointed 'work trustees', the movement sprang to life again spontaneously in many plants as separate groups of workers manifested their own need for workshop organizations. The existence of these councils was legalized by the Control Commission, but with limited advisory functions. It was left to the Federal Republic to establish (albeit reluctantly and only after a threat of a major strike) co-determination in May 1951 and Works Councils in October 1952.

We make these points for two reasons. First, to modify the widespread impression—incidentally held by German employers—that works councils and co-determination were the brain-child of Ernest Bevin, who had still not freed his mind of the syndicalist ideas of workers' control which he had written into the Transport and General Workers' Union's own constitution. Secondly, to emphasize that this movement owes a great deal, if not everything, to the underlying demands of the German workers themselves.

This German example does not support the belief that enforcement of joint consultation would not work in Britain. Only trial and error would ever establish the truth of that. But there is a tradition of voluntary effort in this country, and any such compulsion would be bound initially to meet with hostility from employers and managers. The fact that obligatory joint consultation seems to work tolerably well in nationalized industries only serves to exacerbate opinion in the matter. Furthermore, commentators seem to be divided over the effect upon joint consultative machinery of the growing size of companies and groups. One view is that as the enterprise becomes large and highly centralized, communication becomes more important, and that part of the communication procedure should be works committees. The other view holds that the very size and centralized nature of the enterprise inhibits consultation, which is liable to be slow and clumsy, especially if it bears any decision-making responsibility intended to lead to action. One reason for this is that, in a large production unit, the workers' representatives may find themselves reporting back to as many as sixty people, which can be a practical impossibility.

An answer to the problem that has been found to work is to
split up the business of the works council into self-contained
subjects, such as accident prevention or productivity, and put
it into the hands of a group of standing committees of the
council. The work of such committees can then be reported
upon through the works newspaper, noticeboards, or at special
meetings. Generally speaking, as long as the business of a works
council and its sub-committees is confined to ensuring workers'
co-operation in the more efficient running of the plant under
the direction of management a reasonable and workable procedure can be built up, which can even produce useful results.
But to make it seem worth while both to the managers whose
time is taken up by attendance (and it is in the nature of the
executive life that time away from the desk seems wasted), and
to the shop-floor representatives on to whose shoulders is added
a burden with no financial compensation, the councils and
committees must be seen to do a real job, with obvious, measurable results, such as a reduction in lost-time accidents, a rise in
output and incomes and so on. Oddly enough, rarely is it
suggested that works council representatives should be paid an
honorarium, on the same principle as the payment of Members
of Parliament. Perhaps employers would regard this as piling
Pelion on Ossa: to have workers' participation and pay for it, too!

To sum up the criticisms made by practising Trade Union
officials and managers against formal joint consultation:

(1) Since responsibility for over-all efficiency is disavowed by
most workers and claimed by most managers, such joint consultation is bound to be advisory and cannot be executive. In
consequence, industrial democracy is an irrelevance other than
where responsibility can be equally shared.

(2) People come to value institutions for their own sake and
consequently a movement develops to 'make the Works Council
more effective'. Attempts are then made to endow the Works
Council with an authority and wisdom that is spurious and
mistaken. In this way formal joint consultation becomes more
important than the issues it is meant to resolve. It becomes an
affront to the Works Council to sidetrack it by attempting to
deal with questions as they arise. 'You must work through the
Works Council. If you clear things first with the foreman or
manager the Works Council becomes meaningless, etc., etc.'

(3) Because of (2), middle and first line supervision become

by-passed—yet these are the very levels of management that need bolstering, raising and improving.

(4) Formalized joint consultation thus inhibits the growth and development of *informal* consultation—the informal contact with the men on the shop floor, in the canteen and club, in the street and wherever management and workers can meet whether fortuitously or deliberately to exchange information that can be the prelude to action.

CHAPTER XI

THE TWO SIDES OF INDUSTRY

BRITISH industry has the longest recorded history in the world, and as a consequence has had great difficulty in escaping from tradition. Traditionally there were two sides in industry, the masters, who made the decisions and bore the attendant risks, and the men, who obeyed the decisions and suffered, sometimes more than their masters, when they went wrong. But insecurity of employment has never been regarded as a risk element in business in the same way as entrepreneurial risk taking. Although there are devices to alleviate the results of businessmen's mistakes—limited liability and bankruptcy proceedings, mainly —the only cushion ever provided for the employee until quite recently was unemployment benefit (also a relative newcomer) and even then he had originally met the cost of it himself by deductions from his earnings. Trade union officials have in recent years become quite knowledgeable in the ways of business and the City. They have watched with interest the success with which businesses have failed, leaving the proprietors 'comfortably off', while their erstwhile employees have been laid off at short notice. There are many rifts between the 'two sides', and from either side they look very big indeed.

Many of the old grievances levelled at private enterprise by trade unionists in the 'bad old days' have persisted, either in fact or in the minds of ageing workers who have seen hard times. The Report of the Shipbuilding Inquiry Committee 1965–66, known as the Geddes Report after its chairman, Mr Reay M. Geddes, contains an account of working conditions in this industry which goes a long way towards explaining why it is in such a poor state today.

Being an outdoor industry shipbuilding work is hard, especially in the winter. 'Even that part of it which is under cover takes place mainly in large, lofty sheds which can be difficult to heat and are often noisy. In comfort it is bound to compare unfavourably with work in a factory.' But, the Report adds, it is inherently no worse than, say, the construction industry or, from the noise and hardship point of view, an open steelworks site. Unfortunately, the shipbuilding industry has been very slow to modernize, and a lot of its labour has been drawn off by lighter industries.

Add to this hardship aspect that the industry has a bad record for job security, because of the wide fluctuations in orders and the habit of laying off large numbers of workers at short notice (the Blyth Shipyard gave notice to 1,000 workers in the summer of 1966 while they were away on holiday), and it becomes clearer that the ordinary worker in this industry, even as a new-comer, is bound to pick up the idea that he must make hay while the sun shines. The Geddes Report goes on to say, 'The wide fluctuations in order books and in the level of activity in the yards were met by taking on and putting off labour very often at little more than an hour's notice. The practice was followed by some employers up to the passing of the Contracts of Employment Act in 1963 and even later in some yards for workers not covered by that Act. Further, there was until recently no guarantee of a full week's employment. The past is very much alive in the minds of the workers in the industry and coupled with the general lack of confidence in the future of the industry, it has bred a deep feeling of insecurity which is at the root of most of the demarcation disputes and the practices in the industry which are commonly known as 'restrictive' but which the workers regard as 'protective'.[1]

Such a background would produce embittered relations in any industry, and many industries (as shown in Chapter III) have had a history of poor working conditions and hire and fire that is not so remote that a generation of workers cannot recall it. The evil that companies have done in this way may not live after them, but it certainly dogs them in their efforts to improve. It is not altogether inappropriate, therefore, to refer to the Geddes Report on an old industry where conditions have changed too little for anybody's comfort in order to gauge to some extent how such circumstances affect attitudes on both sides.

Insecurity, the feeling of managerial indifference and even

[1] Cmnd. 2937, p. 97 *et seq*. The long quotation is on p. 103.

callousness, leading to mutual mistrust, coupled with 'protective' inter-union disputes is bound to give rise to strikes, and in this industry the post-war record bears this out. An additional factor pointed out in the Report, and again not unknown in other industries, has been 'a serious lack of any real consultation between them on matters concerning the prosperity of the industry in which both sides have a real identity of interest'. It is this question of identity of interest that is at the heart of the antipathy between management and labour. On the one hand the management declares that there is an identity of interest, but on the other who believes it?

Undoubtedly a leading difficulty in any dispute-prone industry is the inability on the part of the employees to see how their own future prosperity is inevitably bound up with the survival and growth of the companies for which they work. The shipbuilding industry, and other long established industries, may reveal this shortsightedness more than newer 'growth' industries, in which there is no comparable history of friction between the 'two sides', but at the back of the collective mind of labour there may lurk a general and genuine inability to take the broader view.

A Ministry of Labour inquiry into workers' attitudes reported that on the whole, although employees may recognize that their personal effort has something to do with the company's success, they think of their job in much simpler terms. 'Their primary interest is to maximize the wages and other benefits which they derive from their employer. Obviously their ability to do this is conditional on the well-being of the enterprise, but equally the well-being of the enterprise is not their primary object'.[1]

But this self-centred outlook is not exclusively a characteristic of an employee's mentality. There seems to be little identity of interest between management and customers (or consumers), or management and small shareholders, according to the same report, but management must take account of all three, especially if they are inclined to gather into pressure groups, in its conduct of the enterprise, and strive to create as large an area of mutual interest with them as possible. While customers may act as individuals, and shareholders take action hardly at all, employees nowadays tend to behave as groups, whether formal or otherwise, and sometimes overlapping groups as well,

[1] *Attitudes to Efficiency*: a report. Ministry of Labour, 1966.

H

which makes it difficult to determine precisely what their interests really are. The Ministry of Labour report comments: 'From the management point of view the behaviour of employees may often appear unreliable and negative'.

The solution offered by this report may strike managers as unhelpful in the extreme. Having accepted that the responses of the workers are conditioned not only by personal considerations but by the urgings of informal groups and by the rules and customs of formal labour institutions, it must fall to management to develop a 'capacity to analyse correctly a complex situation, in which the management's own involvement makes objective analysis particularly difficult'. But objectivity there must be, and this is not an easy state of mind to achieve where other parties to a dispute appear to be behaving impulsively and illogically. It has, however, to be recognized that every decision that a management makes and acts upon creates a new set of conditions that may, in turn, produce new problems. *Ad hoc* solutions are to be avoided, for too often they turn out to be no more than temporary palliatives that cannot put right a fundamentally uneasy state of affairs.

The objective analysis, therefore, has to be comprehensive and long-term, making the objectives of the company as clear as possible to everyone who works in it. It follows, or it should follow, that the number of unexpected labour relations situations can in this way be reduced, and that when the unexpected does occur, there is an agreed and satisfactory policy for dealing with it. Also, if the objectives of the company are made known and are accepted, the actions taken to achieve them are more likely to gain acceptance too. This may imply a greater use of joint consultation than some managements are prepared for. And, of course, in companies where the proprietor or a small and related group of proprietors runs the whole show, it may prove impossible to set objectives far enough ahead to make full use of this kind of scheme. The planning concept (whether it be a manpower plan that takes account of future recruitment needs and wastage, or a productivity agreement keyed to a profit plan) is still new in Britain, and the mass of smaller, proprietorial firms has yet to show either interest or enthusiasm for it.

Some of the larger companies, on the other hand, have taken to what has become known as corporate planning. It is an all-embracing system of setting targets for stated periods ahead, five to ten years is already customary among large American companies, and then plotting the necessary courses of action. Naturally the success of such long-range planning depends in part, if not wholly, on preserving good labour relations, and one method of achieving this particular objective is to build into the plan with the help of the trade unions some kind of 'escalator agreement' on wages, such as exists between the Ford Motor Company in the United States and the Automobile Workers Union. Even with the British motor industry's two dozen unions it should be possible to settle on a plan for hours and wages, but at present any such constructive step seems very remote. If there were one union for the industry, the chances of success would be infinitely greater, but the attitudes of the two sides of this industry is not at bottom so very different from those recorded in the Geddes Report for the older industry with a tougher and far less affluent environment.

But it needs to be said that while a greater degree of integration and amalgamation within the trade union structure is desirable for itself, if only for the sake of organizational efficiency, this is no more likely to produce a better spirit in industrial relations than any other similar change. Equally, a lengthening of the intervals between the re-opening of negotiations concerning the basic contract could, in theory, conduce to greater stability. Yet there are pitfalls here too. Just as the single, monolithic organization tends to concentrate too much power in the hands of the leaders at the centre, so too does the concentration of negotiating activity at a single point in time, that is separated from the previous negotiations by a long interval, tend to leave too much to be decided on that occasion. Issues tend to build up over the period and the consequent bill that has to be met is often too great for an industry or, indeed, an economy, to digest at that time. The resulting dissatisfaction could well be explosive. Human nature being what it is and subject, as McGregor has shown, to an unfolding and developing series of wants, suggests that there is much to be said for regarding 'labour relations' as a continuing activity that requires unremitting attention rather than otherwise. It is not a matter that can be conveniently swept under the carpet for twelve to twenty-four months at a time.

A reduction in the number of trade unions in an industry is

unquestionably an improvement, but it gives greater opportunities for the emphasis to swing from left to right and back again as leadership changes hands in the more tightly controlled trade unions. There have been many occasions in the United Kingdom during the post-war years when the whole political outlook of an entire trade union has changed, merely because of a change in the general secretaryship.

Graham Turner, in his 'panoramic' study, *The Car Makers*,[1] points to the industry's terrible record of strikes but reminds us that not one of the hundreds of disputes arose from an attempt to cut wages, which have risen steadily since the war, to the extent that many of the workers in the industry have developed individually what he terms a new middle-class pattern of living based on high take-home pay (with a lot of overtime) and hire purchase. Their middle-class mentality does not apparently extend, however, much beyond the attainment of a high standard of living, otherwise one might expect that they and their representatives, the shop stewards, would more often see eye to eye with management.

The gap between the two sides in the motor industry comes across vividly in the series of reports issued by the Motor Industry Joint Labour Council between November 1965 and August 1966. On the the Rover Company Assembly Works dispute the Council commented that although relations seemed basically satisfactory and working conditions quite reasonable there had been 126 stoppages between June 1964 and October 1965, mostly concerned with pay or matters affecting the level of earnings. Yet management 'apparently believed itself confronted by a situation explainable only in psychological terms and failed to get down to a close analysis of specific causes and motivations'. The Council added that it considered that management had been slack about communication and consultation, partly because of personality problems. In fact senior shop stewards had been by-passing the Joint Management and Shop Stewards Committee and management had allowed them to do so, instead of reconstituting the committee and making it work. There were also signs of management resentment at the apparent impossibility of making quick and constructive

[1] 1963. There is a chapter on labour relations in the industry and chapters on Vauxhall and Ford, the one peaceful, the other riven with disputes. This contrast no longer exists.

decisions at shop-floor level between foremen and shop stewards. The report naturally made its No. 1 recommendation a revision of the consultative procedure.

At Morris Bodies in Coventry the Council's report on a dispute over the introduction of measured day work and the use of work measurement as part of the system led to, among others, a comment that 'There is at present a lack of understanding of the company's intentions which has given rise to a great deal of suspicion'. Otherwise relations in the factory were good enough for progress to be made. On the piece-work dispute at Standard-Triumph the report eventually asks for management-union co-operation to achieve productivity and for 'a joint approach carried out in an atmosphere of mutual understanding'.

It is little short of remarkable that so little progress has been made in so many industries towards bridging this communication gap. Certainly there is evidence that in some instances representatives of management have made hasty and ill-considered announcements which have sparked off on-the-spot disputes that have eventually led to unofficial stoppages if not strikes. There is also the consideration that on the shop-floor in some industries with a 'tough' tradition there is profound mistrust of management. Put the two factors together and trouble is bound to follow.

Among management's many responsibilities must be included the willingness to allay suspicion by complete and well-timed policy statements. Naturally it is also a step towards mutual confidence if responsible representatives of the workpeople take a hand in the forming of policy as it will impinge upon them. One of the most important aspects of the gap in understanding between management and labour emerges in an examination of traditional attitudes and of what one side expects from the other.

In an interesting article in *International Management*,[1] Mr A. J. M. Sykes of the University of Strathclyde, Glasgow, has to some extent succeeded in assessing what these expectations are. The employers claim the right to private property, the right of private enterprise and the right to loyalty from their employees. Mr Sykes takes these 'rights' and examines the workers'

[1] 1965–66, 'The Ideological Basis of Industrial Relations in Great Britain', pp. 65–72.

attitudes to them. On the first he finds that the right to personal property is well established but that 'the right to private property on a large scale is not fully accepted'. It follows, therefore, that although the workers recognize the employers' powers as owners of the places where they work, they believe them to be limited by four other 'rights' of their own: the right to work; the right to share in profits; the right to be consulted on working conditions; and the right to challenge any rules or regulations thought up by the employer or the management which the workers consider to be unfair or contrary to established custom.

The first 'right' has given rise to the now accepted national economic policy of full employment, although opinions may differ as to what in practice constitutes 'full' in this connection. The second 'right' is more contentious but plays an important part in trade union thinking, inasmuch as there now exists a firmly rooted belief that wages should increase as the profitability of an industry or a company increases. In 1956, for example, the Amalgamated Engineering Union resolved at a delegate meeting that its members should share in the increased productivity and profits that would accrue from automation. The other two 'rights' are part and parcel of the negotiable areas that have come to be recognized by most employers and all trade unions over the years.

In addition to these there has now grown up a claim on the part of organized labour that a worker has a form of property right in a particular job, not merely the right to work at any kind of work or in his particular skill in any job he can get. It is this proprietory claim to a job that has led to inter-union clashes over demarcation lines between craft skills, and such disputes go a long way to confirm employers, managers and the general public in the opinion that workers and trade unionists in particular are impulsive, erratic and irresponsible.

When it comes to the employers' 'rights', some of the gaps in understanding appear to be wide indeed. First, there is the private enterprise outlook or philosophy, which holds that freedom of action is essential to the proper conduct of business and that trade union activities are a restriction on this freedom. As Sykes points out, trade unionism can also be seen as a restriction upon the freedom of the individual worker, especially where there is a 'closed shop' or where expulsion from the union means loss of employment. From the conventional employer's viewpoint the individual must make his own way; he has a right to prosper by his own efforts. This is not compatible with collective bargaining. But the unions are able to point to a long history of success in making gains for their members by united action that the individual worker could never have made on his own.

On the question of loyalty, opinion is sharply divided with employers tending to believe that a worker owes loyalty to them and to the companies of which they are founders or chairmen. The company provides a man with his living and in return expects loyalty and obedience, within reason, and even that the individual should put the company's well-being before his own, for without it he loses his livelihood. Therefore he should respond to the company's demands before those of his trade union. This is the exact opposite of the workers' thinking. The unions are inclined to argue that workers do not owe any loyalty to the employers, who hire and fire labour as they please and generally build no lasting bond between 'capital' and 'labour'. As Sykes phrases it, the worker can identify with his union much more readily than he can with his place of work because 'The union is truly "his", but the place of work remains his employer's'.

Most industrial disputes stem from these conflicts of rights and loyalties, so unless they are clearly understood and evaluated by both sides mutual understanding is bound to remain an impossibility. The very fact that management, which is becoming increasingly 'professional' and detached from direct pecuniary interest in the profitability of the firm and the ownership of the assets, occupies a central position between owner and employee ought to make it easier for it to adopt an objective standpoint. But in order to achieve such an ideal frame of mind it must first come to grips with the workers' modes of thought and then interpret their actions in the light of this general background and of the particular circumstances of the place and type of work.

In his almost unique study, *On the Shopfloor*, Professor Tom Lupton has pointed out that misunderstandings between workers and management often derive from 'a discrepancy between two logics'. Management thinking is largely based on the logic of efficiency, while in most cases the workers' logic, because they are 'groupish' and cling to custom and tradition, is a logic of sentiment. 'This is why their reactions so often seem to be irrational and so exasperating to management'.[1]

In working towards the improvement of labour relations in any workplace management has therefore got to make the attempt to see the ordinary worker's point of view, as a vulnerable, cautious, naturally suspicious but also potentially loyal individual.

[1] 1963, p. 6.

CHAPTER XII

ANY ANSWERS?

In a short while we shall be reaching the centenary of the passing by Parliament of 34 & 35 Victoria cap. 31, better known as the Trade Union Act, 1871, and the first real step on the road to modern trade union power. Will anyone be celebrating this historical occasion? Or are we all now so remote from the spirit of that time that 1871 hardly strikes us as a great event any more?

It has been said many a time by disgruntled employers and members of the general public who have felt themselves inflicted with hardship by apparently unnecessary strikes that the trade unions today have too much power and that from this strength they wage economic war on their own behalf against whomsoever happens to get in their way. There have been times when the situation must have seemed very much like that to outsiders, watching a great industry riven with conflict, losing business, wasting assets, running down the country's export effort, only to conclude with a settlement not noticeably different from that proposed at the outset.

In their study, *Labour Relations in the Motor Industry*, Professor H. A. Turner and his two co-authors[1] have been driven to the conclusion that 'the recent strike-proneness of the British car industry . . . reflects a failure of institutions', with a parenthesis to the effect that they see no reason to think that their conclusion may not be more generally applicable. In short, the troubles that have been besetting Britain's biggest industry (an industry upon which the economy now appears to pivot) arise not from poor human relations created by its peculiar technological setting; nor from 'automation', whatever that may be taken to mean; nor from geographical isolation; nor from working conditions; nor 'green labour'; nor agitators; nor shop stewards; nor low morale. The car industry's strike-proneness, in the

[1] Garfield Clack and Geoffrey Roberts, 1967.

opinion of three assiduous and thoughtful scholars whose views have been cross-checked in the industry itself, arises from the failure of both the employers' associations and the trade unions (as well as the companies themselves) either to understand their predicament as a strike-prone industry or to cope with it. This conclusion, which is most carefully presented and explained, leads them to make certain recommendations about the adaptation of both unions and employers' organizations (in this instance the Engineering Employers' Federation) which amount to reshaping them to meet the special needs of the industry, one of which is 'parallel unionism' or the unofficial system of representation noticed earlier in this book, which always arises when the traditional or conventional system proves itself less than adequate.

Whether this conclusion be well-founded or not is less important than the comment that, while it is of the broadest practical significance for British industry as a whole, 'it was, of course, just this one which was least likely to be picked out by the "official" methods of examination largely adopted', because such inquiries tend to be dominated by the specific incidents preceding them. Indeed, one might go further and add that all too rarely is any thinking done on the question of labour disputes that rises above the current conflict and looks for less immediate and observable causes.

It was never the purpose of this small book to usurp the role of seer and problem-solver for the trade unions and employers of Britain, but to set out in an accessible form an array of the thinking and action that have paved the road to present industrial relations. By charting this route as objectively as possible it was hoped that managers not wholly familiar with all the ramifications of the trade union story would be provided with useful background knowledge, forewarned about other people's theories and explanations and left to continue their own thinking in the context of reality.

The last two or three years have seen both unions and management bombarded with advice from all sides, culminating with the Royal Commission on Trade Unions and Employers' Organizations, which must have collected together every last scrap of systematic thinking on every aspect of British industrial relations, supplemented by material from overseas. But while the Royal Commission has been deliberating there have been scores of utterances, both critical and polemical, from the raucous *Daily Mirror* pamphlet 'Trade Unions—Time to take off the Blinkers' to the NEDO's quiet but firm rap on management's knuckles in the *Ministry of Labour Gazette*, 'Labour Utilization'.[1]

The IPM journal *Personnel Management* asked, in September 1965, 'Why not Teach more Industrial Relations?' a subject which, said Mr Alan Marsh, 'is usually on the very edge of management education', because the handling of people at work is not central to the conventional pattern of management studies. Nor does it look like becoming so, with pressure from the newer, high-level business education centres to make managers 'numerate' taking priority over the behavioural sciences. There is, in addition, the now well-rooted belief that 'personnel management' is a separate skill best exercised by trained specialists. This belief has done considerable harm to labour-management relations by allowing line managers to continue in ignorance of their own need to study, understand and apply what small amount of systematic knowledge exists. In the circumstances, when a lecturer in trade union studies says that courses in his subject are indispensable for managers, and that they must also be long enough to go adequately into its subtleties if they are to do any good, there is likely to be as much amused scepticism as genuine acceptance. The specialist advisers to industry are all, for various reasons, enthusiasts about their particular interests. But there have been signs in the last ten years that some sectors of industry have had too many disappointments on the side of non-technical advice (meaning the human sciences and managerial side rather than the technological). A certain coolness towards conferences and courses is only to be expected, especially as they do not appear to change radically in material or presentation, but continue to consist either of cautious speeches about accomplishments or lectures concocted from cases and tentative conclusions.

This is not to say that such educational activity should not continue, only that it should become more practical, helpful and plain spoken. For too long there has been a tendency to minimize the labour-management tensions in industry, to pretend that in fact there are not 'two sides' with differing aims and outlooks, and by sheer exhortation to hope to abolish the

[1] October 25–28, 1965: October 1966.

greatest gulf of all in British industry—the one that yawns between those who own and run industry, and those who work for them for the lowest pay, doing the physically harder jobs.

The nature of this gulf can be judged by comparing attitudes. Take redundancy, for example, which, although it sometimes affects individual managers, generally affects workers by hundreds at least. In a certain engineering company, a rare event took place. A man in his fifties reached the managing director's chair after fifteen years with the firm, beginning as a fitter and machine operator. One of his early suggestions was for a redundancy scheme to be established. His boardroom colleagues immediately protested that there was no redundancy, times were good, and so forth. To which this unusual managing director, who knew personally what it felt like on the shop floor, replied that this was the right time to plan for it, and not to wait until there was neither the time nor the money to operate a sufficiently generous scheme.

There are two aspects to such a gesture. There is the danger that the announcement of a redundancy scheme may be taken as an early sign that the company expects to be in trouble (or the possibility that the unions, once they are convinced that no actual redundancies are contemplated, may consider the scheme just so much window-dressing). And there is the need for the scheme not to be reduced in anybody's mind to the level of a gesture, a perfunctory 'good time' arrangement that costs nothing to announce, and which takes its place alongside the house magazine, the company annual outing and the works social club as just another of management's condescensions.

There has, in the not so distant past, and probably still if all the facts were known, been deep disappointment on the part of nice-minded employers with their workpeople's reaction to generosity—the neglect of the sports club, the poorly attended social functions, the house magazines thrown away on the day of issue (and agonies of indecision over the reason—would people have read it had it not been free, etc.?), the new washrooms left in a filthy condition, and even damaged, the posters defaced, the safety clothing unworn, the machines damaged by careless use (or apparent sabotage, perish the thought), the general bad behaviour and, of course, the rising sickness absence rate as soon as a sick-pay scheme is put in, not to mention the ultimate betrayal, the prompt sale of any transferable company shares that may have been issued under a co-partnership agreement.

Such things do not happen all the time, of course, nor in some firms do they happen at all, but they have all happened somewhere at some time, or variations of them, and quite often they have been ascribed to such indefinable causes as 'bloody-mindedness', 'bolshy behaviour', 'vandalism', 'hooliganism', a whole vocabulary of smoke-screen words. But in fact all such happenings are straws in a much bigger wind, as most industrial psychologists, some sociologists and probably all personnel managers would agree, with greater or less emphasis. For these signals of discontent, uneasiness, unhappiness, low morale, call it what you will, are the surface tension of a deep-seated, semi-conscious antagonism, a conflict of interests. Consider how often you will hear employers and managers talking privately about the concept of profit, and how misunderstood it is on the shop floor. It is true that a company which fails to earn a profit faces eventual complete failure. But consider, too, how difficult it is to ascertain readily the true profitability of a company, if that company is pursuing a 'conservative' accounting policy—depreciating its assets, building up reserves, attributing generous overheads. Some trade unions make an attempt to gauge the profitability of companies or even of whole industries in order to pursue 'just' pay claims, on the basis of fair shares or, more sophisticated, of surplus value. Seldom are their calculations well received.

Employers and managers are apt to look upon such financial intelligence gathering as a kind of snooping or spying. They know well enough that unions become shareholders so that they can have access to the annual report and accounts and attend the Annual General Meeting. Not many unions do this yet, apparently, so it seems equally unlikely that they would follow the action through to its logical conclusion and communicate to those members who happen to work for the company under scrutiny the true commercial standing that it enjoys so that they might act accordingly. In other words, even when the knowledge of a company's economic strengths or weaknesses is made available (as with certain newspaper companies in recent years) there seems to be no inclination for the people on the payroll to regard their actions as in any way connected with its survival or growth. This is the outward and visible sign of the 'interest gap' identified in Chapter XI that lies at the heart of so many differences and disputes. The unions pursue short-term gains at the expense of long-term security. The managements keep their inside knowledge and their problems to themselves until it is too late for their confidences to look anything more than a last-minute appeal to the unions for help and co-operation that could have been earned. We cannot simply write this off as another example of the clash between 'management logic' and the 'sentiment-based logic' of workpeople.[1] This is not a clash between two logics, but between two attitudes and, when it comes down to the root of the matter, between two classes with divergent interests—or perhaps one should say apparently divergent interests, because the enterprise in the end is the goose that lays the golden eggs for everybody.

The enterprise, the profit-making entity, is the bone of contention, even when it ceases to be a private firm and becomes a public corporation. But there is an important difference between these two, as regards attitudes to enterprise and profit-making which, we are told, is the realistic purpose of business, the *raison d'être* of the business organization, and that is accountability. The public corporation (in the British sense of a nationalized industry) is publicly accountable, the private company is not, in spite of (or because of) the state of company law, though it may be a little more on show now the law relating to company operations is amended. There is an undoubted mystique about the financial control and limited accountability of a public joint stock company, and more so about the affairs of a private company—the majority of businesses in this country. It has been said that directors, managers, shareholders and even the Fraud Squad have difficulty in grasping the full import of some of the subtler financial points at issue. Exaggerations apart, there is little doubt that enlightened management is right to assume that the finer points of balance sheet and profit and loss account are a closed ledger to the man-in-the-street, let alone the man on the shop floor. As we have seen, attempts have been made to water down the technicalities and spell out in simple terms the 'facts' about a company's operations so that the worker, who may be no fool at the intricacies of pool dividends and racetrack odds, should have a chance to calculate for himself that his take-home pay is at least reasonable. It does

[1] Lupton, *op. cit.*, p. 6.

not seem to have worked, not because too few companies made the effort (some go on trying), but because the whole exercise looks like and is regarded as window-dressing.

Had the information not come via the accountants' office and the Board Room through management's 'communication' system, but direct from a Board member elected to observe and speak up for the shop floor, it might have been received with less indifference and cynicism. It is no part of the purpose of this book to proffer solutions to problems, but there exists the interesting alternative in this connection between the further nationalization of enterprise and what George Goyder has called 'the further evolution of the limited liability company as a corporate body to embrace the wills and needs of all its participants, and not merely those of the shareholders'.[1]

It is not only a question of intelligent participation in the life and future of the company. Alongside this time-honoured and cherished idea that still has to be properly tried out in this country stands the equally traditional but lately resuscitated concept of the worker's 'rights' in his job, which are subtly different from the older concept of a 'right to work'. The right to work, which loosely interpreted means no more than the chance of a job if a job is available, has come to be inextricably associated in Britain with full employment and the determination of the labour movement, both economic and political, to preserve a situation where involuntary unemployment is held to a minimum. But, as Professor K. W. Wedderburn says in *The Worker and the Law*,[2] 'Before "propertylike" guarantees can be won by workers today, the industry needs to be confident of its economic future'. Thus, once again the interdependence of capital and labour, so much lauded by the mid-Victorian conformist trade unionist and so held up to ridicule by extremists, is shown to persist. There is no doubt that reasonable people feel that, as Sir George Pollock of the quondam British Employers' Confederation said in a letter to *The Times* (April 30, 1964), although a man cannot expect to hold a vested interest in a particular job, he certainly has some stake in a company or an industry to which he has devoted a large part of his working life. And while this may have nothing much to do with formal trade union organization as we understand it today, no one

---

[1] *Responsible Company*, 1961, p. 127.
[2] 1965, pp. 95–6.

would deny that it is one of the fundamental ideas underlying many of the thoughts and actions of trade unionists and socialists in the past century and a half. *The Times* Labour Correspondent, E. L. Wigham, a member of the Royal Commission on Trade Unions' and Employers' Associations pointed out in a 'turnover' article (July 15, 1966) that the Minister of Labour, Mr Ray Gunter, had said something very similar in introducing the Redundancy Payments Act, to the effect that a man has rights in his job in the same way as an employer has rights in his property. As Mr Wigham went on to reason, this carries the management-labour relationship much further than a contract of employment. It carries it to the point where the management-worker-shareholder relationship and balance of interests may need to be re-thought. This, it seems, is what the Labour Party study group on workers' participation and industrial democracy set out to do. This approach is radically different from the more familiar one that argues that industrial discipline stems from management's ability and freedom to apply sanctions, and that this ability is strengthened in times of high unemployment, which confers on management a freedom lacking in a situation of full employment. Whether it is true that worker representation is 'patently, a very important confidence factor in shaping the response of the unions' hardly seems to call for argument.[1] Enlightened managements already see the value of this. It is not to enlightened managements that this small book is addressed.

[1] *Industrial Democracy* (Labour Party, 1967), p. 45.

INDUSTRIAL RELATIONS

AUTHORS' NOTE

THE following three case histories, considerably abbreviated from the original documents, are offered as examples of successful procurement or change by managements. The essential ingredients for bringing about change in industrial practices and outlook include:

1. A management that is satisfied that change is desirable and justifiable. Such a change (in structure, in numbers, in working practices, etc.) can be introduced in a controlled manner and with less adverse effect on employees than if any attempt to change or adapt were neglected up to the point where it became inevitable and therefore uncontrollable. Management needs to manage in terms of tomorrow as well as today.

2. A management that is determined to manage and not to abdicate its responsibility. One of the more flabby attitudes that has been evinced by managements in the post-war era is that a change could not be brought about 'because the unions would not stand for it'. While it seems to be true that the trade unions in Britain are not notable for their capacity to change, they cannot be entirely to blame for this outlook, which sometimes appears to be an alibi for management's own inactivity. One of the most encouraging aspects of the three cases that follow is the revelation of trade union readiness to accept change when it is wisely introduced and skilfully negotiated.

3. A management that sees that the peripheral communication of what is planned is more important to the success of planned change than the central. In the last resort what happens on the shop floor determines whether a change is accepted or not. Trade union officials and managers are too inclined to believe that what has been negotiated at the centre is crucial, while those on the extremes need only to be told about it.

Slowly, but much too slowly, it is coming to be realized as a consequence of projects such as the Fawley 'Blue Book', SPEAR and the Milton Plan that the people on the shop floor have a right to know what is planned for them by management. And this applies to clerical staff, supervision and junior management as well. Successful change is the outcome of complete and open communication, within the limits of business exigency (a condition that must not be abused), and communication is a give-and-take exercise that involves everyone in the organization from the boardroom to the shop floor.

I

PRODUCTIVITY BARGAINING

THE productivity bargain struck in 1960 at the Fawley Refinery of the Esso Petroleum company was perhaps the most significant change in the management approach to collective bargaining that had been made by any company since 1945. Such 'in-plant' agreements between local managements and representatives of labour have since spread to other oil refineries, to the electricity supply industry and have also been tried out in the engineering industry, but with less happy results. Subsequently arguments have been advanced against them, in spite of the palpable gains in labour productivity that they can be observed to bring, the main one being that the increased earnings that result tend to be disruptive of wage negotiations elsewhere and of national wage agreements in industries.

Essentially, the productivity bargain is the trading of higher rates of pay for the workers in a plant in exchange for the cessation of restrictive practices and usually of overtime, it being now generally recognized that most overtime is inessential and has arisen through the continual shortening of the working week and the willingness of employers to bargain for labour outside the standard hourly rates that have been agreed industrially.

The Fawley operation has been held up as a shining example of initiative and common sense, coupled with carefully planned communication of concessions and demands with the object of avoiding the all too common misunderstanding of intentions that so often accompanies such moves by management. There is naturally almost always a lurking suspicion that management is 'pulling a fast one'.

For this reason the document that came to be known as the Fawley 'Blue Book' is central to the scheme. Its official title is significant, *High Productivity and High Wages at Fawley*, and it contains a number of policy statements that underline the thinking behind its production and contents. One paragraph reads:

> Management has a duty to see that productivity is improved so that higher rates of pay do not lead to higher prices. Management can sometimes provide the opportunity for such an improvement, but the level of productivity often depends on the attitude of the man on the job. The ordinary union member can play a very real part merely by the attitude he has to his work.

Flanders points out in his detailed account of the reception of the Blue Book, and the lengthy negotiations that followed, the initial suspicion and hostility with which the document was received, and the widespread impression that here was a comprehensive list of management's demands that would be pushed through as completely as possible. The Amalgamated Engineering Union's District Committee 'which had no member employed at the refinery and was strongly influenced by traditional craft union sentiment in Southampton' was the most hostile of all the unions involved and went as far as to break off discussions with the company after hearing a report of a branch meeting at which the majority present were against the Blue Book. At this early stage the whole scheme might have stalled, had the refinery management displayed impatience at this offhand reception of its already protracted labours.

To grasp what was at stake it is necessary to know the bare outline of what the Blue Book offered and expected in return. In sum, Esso was offering 2,400 earners roughly a 40 per cent increase to be spread over two years in return for concessions that included cutting the working week to 40 hours, reducing overtime from 18 to 2 per cent, relaxing many of the demarcation rules between trades that hampered maintenance work, abolishing 'walking time', 'washing time' and similar unproductive traditions (they took up three and a half hours a week), and dispensing with the 300 'mates who accompanied the 500 craftsmen in their work, 120 of them to be upgraded to skilled status by re-training. These items, plus management's demand to be allowed more freedom in the use of supervisors (there were five grades originally, from leading hand to assistant mechanical superintendent) in order to reduce the hierarchy from six levels, including the head of department, to four, were the core of the Blue Book negotiations.

During the first two years these negotiations produced a 50 per cent increase in productivity among maintenance workers. The maintenance crews' average weekly hours were reduced from 50 hours to 42½. Process productivity went up 45 per cent, and overtime fell in the Process Department from 17 to 10.5 per cent. Hourly earnings rose by an average of 35 per cent, compared with a 20 per cent increase during the period for the rest of the oil industry. Best of all for the refinery management, by the end of 1962 there was £12 million more investment in plant at Fawley compared with 1959, but it was being operated by a small labour force—2,266 as against 2,461.

As far as workplace efficiency is concerned, the gains obtained by the Fawley Refinery management are a landmark of encouragement in the rather barren scene of labour productivity in post-war Britain. Professor Hugh Clegg has summed up the mounting overtime problem as the working week has shortened in a pamphlet written for the British Institute of Management, *Implications of the Shorter Working Week for Management*,[1] in which he records that 'large sections of British workers are taught by their system of payment to waste time at work'. He also makes the telling point that it is of little use for management to insist on efficient employment of other resources, machines, raw materials and so on, if simultaneously thousands of hours of skilled labour time are being systematically wasted. A number of writers, including Clegg and Flanders, have commented upon the way in which this customary overtime-working cuts into the leisure time of workers. Nevertheless, it seems that the initiative to dispense with it as an anti-social as well as an uneconomic practice must still come from management.

The inertia of habit and custom in the labour movement is illustrated in another way by the Fawley negotiations. Even after the acceptance by the unions of a large part of the Blue Book proposals, the suggestion that 120 craftsmen's mates should be upgraded was rejected by all the craft unions except the Electrical Trades Union. About a dozen mates were subsequently accorded craft status. This upgrading and the relaxation of demarcation rules were both departures from tradition, as was the withdrawal of mates. The last, says Flanders, 'was accomplished with little or no resentment from the craftsmen, whilst every measure of greater flexibility that touched their

[1] Occasional Paper No. 8, 1961.

work was subjected to the most careful scrutiny'. Eventually the proposals in the Blue Book concerning inter-craft flexibility had to be modified in negotiation.

As might be expected, the firmest resistance to the withdrawal of mates (who were members of the Transport and General Workers' Union) came from the mates themselves, who, until they received proof positive that they were not just being 'thrown on the scrap heap', felt that they were being treated as 'poor relations' and that their craftsmen colleagues were indifferent to their fate.

The unskilled worker faces a tough problem if he becomes ambitious to be upgraded to craft status. The craft unions, to membership of which he must aspire if he is to work in a trade, resist 'dilution' firmly, and endeavour for the most part to admit to their ranks only those men who have 'served their time'. It is now generally admitted (though not officially by the craft unions) that the long token apprenticeship is out of date, wasteful and restrictive. Apart from the evident fact that a trade can be learned in a much shorter time than the unions insist upon, the technical frontiers of the trades themselves have been growing vaguer and therefore increasingly inappropriate for some time. Clashes between trade unions over what we now refer to as 'demarcation' are analogous to frontier clashes between young nation states over arbitrarily delineated boundaries: between what each would regard as its 'natural' frontier lies an area of dispute that neither will willingly concede. Flanders says that the craft attitude goes further than this, demanding in effect that not only must the craft unions' 'frontiers' be preserved but that trespassers must be repulsed and more 'ground' gained if possible. Behind this apparent niggling over minor rights and traditions lies the collective fear that the identity of the craft may be undermined and eventually destroyed. Such an attitude augurs ill for the advancement of technical change in industries that are largely dependent on skilled, organized labour.

It was to face up to this that the Fawley management devised the Blue Book and its subsequent negotiation procedure. The danger lay not merely in the ingrained mistrust of a management bearing gifts, or rather making offers, but of the unionists' awareness that anything conceded within a single works or plant site might have wider consequences in other places and other industries, and that their fellow-craftsmen might one day

1*

make accusations that the Fawley men had 'sold the pass'. Looked at from the point of view of the Esso management (and of management in general) the widening of the positive influence of the Fawley settlement can be seen as an essential part of the preservation of a productivity agreement. One isolated instance has less chance of survival than the first of a series of such agreements that will strengthen each other and gradually permeate industry as a whole. That was one of the many predictions made about the Esso experiment, which at the same time was denounced here and there by other employers as 'soft' and over-conciliatory. We have to remember that there still exists in Britain a 'tough' school of management, one element of which still basically believes that trade union intransigence is born of full employment. Since the first heartwarming, optimism-stimulating impact of Fawley, antagonists have been heard to use the word 'bribes' of the concessions so carefully defined and calculated by the Esso managers. It is a salutary reminder that in the present state of British industrial relations emotive and abusive terminology is still to be heard, echoing attitudes formed two generations ago.

The Esso management itself proceeded to try and widen the scope of its productivity agreement by bringing in its distributive workers. Significantly, in order to arrive at a progressive arrangement with the chief union involved, the T and GWU, Esso felt obliged to resign from its membership of the Oil Companies' Conciliation Committee.[1] Within this committee they saw little or no prospect of making any progress towards better utilization of assets (for example, speeding up truck driving from the union maximum of 30 m.p.h. to the legal limit of 40), which could also lead to higher rewards for employees if properly handled. The labour agreement for which the OCCC was responsible, was, of course, industry-wide and the Esso proposals were intended to affect one company alone. To obtain this departure from tradition a break with the Committee was an essential preliminary move, and the union was in agreement with this view. More than that the union made a point of saying that they, too, wanted to reduce overtime—'a social and industrial evil'. One union leader even said that Esso had been the first company to come forward with a plan. In the outcome, after much hard bargaining a five-point scheme or 'new deal'

[1] *Esso Magazine*, Spring 1966, p. 12.

was arrived at, comprising the usual constituents of a productivity agreement: reduction in grading divisions; a guaranteed, basic forty-hour week; a basic wage for this week, removing the complexities of overtime and driving bonuses; target setting to establish when wage increases should be paid for higher productivity; and a redundancy scheme to cope with those employees made surplus by higher efficiency.

The way to this agreement was by no means smooth, and the company had to give way over a number of objectives, like Sunday working and the use of tachographs on the lorries to measure journeys. In the end the new deal was a compromise (one depot hung the negotiations out for a further year) but achieved the main aim of the negotiations as far as the company was concerned, to put the payment of Esso drivers, mates and ancillaries in distribution on a rational footing, paying more for a basic week of actual work, rather than paying apparently less for a shift system heavily loaded with overtime.

The report of the National Board of Prices and Incomes[1] has summed up the general results of seven famous productivity agreements concluded in Britian in the past seven or eight years. So far there is no evidence that a genuine productivity agreement has an upward influence on general wage levels (although the Board issued a warning against negotiators trying to tempt union representatives with 'extravagant levels of pay which would provoke resentment outside'). The economic objective of an agreement should be a contribution to lower or stable prices, says the Report, which may be thought to set rather too ideal a standard. To secure any improvement in productivity in an age of restrictive practices is an achievement in itself. The main difficulty appears to lie in the convincing o the trade unions involved that the object is greater efficiency for the survival and future growth of the enterprise, to the advantage of both parties to the bargain, and not merely another capitalist ruse to get more work for the same pay, or more simply just a matter of the business, from which the worker is excluded as a legal participant, looking after its corporate self. It is not a matter of the altruism of management, and rarely has been in the history of private enterprise. If greater efficiency can be gained by give and take it is up to management to arrange it. And as long as the trade unions are content to leave it at that,

[1] No. 36 *Productivity Agreements*, Cmnd. 3311, 1967.

they will have two main alternatives, to co-operate or to obstruct. Where, in their wisdom, they opt for the positive rather than the negative choice their members will benefit, not temporarily but in the long-term. For the furtherance of the usiness (no matter how disproportionate the rewards to nanagement and risk-bearers may appear), can only mean in the end the furtherance of the interests of those who are part of it.

It is significant that in 1967 an official investigation of productivity agreements in British industry should be able to mention no more than fifteen examples, although the record shows that they have brought positive and lasting gains. But one of the chief reasons for the slowness with which management has been able to take advantage of a method that is basically only a rearrangement of contractual terms within a locality or a trade group lies outside management's direct control. The Prices and Incomes Board report says[1]: 'Productivity agreements place a special strain upon internal union communications. In the end the agreements will only work if they are accepted by the men who are asked to make radical changes in their habits and methods of work. This presents the union with a problem, but also with an opportunity for reforming methods of communication which were already unsatisfactory'.

[1] Cmnd. 3311, pp. 28–9.

THE SPEAR PROJECT

THE letters stand for Steel, Peech Electric Arc Reorganization. This was a five-year technical changeover at the steel firm of Steel, Peech and Tozer, Sheffield and Rotherham, a member of the United Steel group of companies, and now nationalized.

The object was to replace twenty-one open-hearth melting furnaces with six arc furnaces, raising the output of the company's furnace capacity from 1,100,000 ingot tons a year to 1,350,000 ingot tons. In the course of this change it was known well in advance that about 900 men would have to be redeployed, retrained or made redundant. The handling of this drastic reorganization was so exemplary that is was thought worth while to allot a brief description of it as an appendix to this book.

The largest electric steel-making plant in the world, which was what the shop at Rotherham became when the scheme was completed in February 1965, began life when approval was given to its plans in July 1959. Before that date, however, the scheme to deal with the people involved had already been drafted. It was estimated that more than 900 would be affected, that some of them would become redundant and that a number of others would have to be down-graded and would lose pay. A senior manager was detached to investigate this problem alone. The human side of the changeover was not going to be dealt with as merely one aspect of the project, but as a problem important enough in itself to warrant special handling.

The first decision was that long-term employees would be found work elsewhere in the company or the group (one of the advantages of size in such circumstances). Also compensation terms were worked out for employees whose earning power was likely to be reduced. About fourteen months before work on the furnace site was timed to begin, a series of meetings was held with middle management (departmental heads) to whom the project and the redeployment plans were outlined. These managers then passed this background information on to their own staffs at further meetings. At each stage questions and answers were freely exchanged.

The next stage was a meeting of the foremen's council and the staff council, and the representatives who attended these were asked to hold reporting back meetings with their 'constituents'. Then came a meeting of the works council and the trades union officers. Questioning on redundancy was close and detailed, and a further meeting had to be arranged to clear up the details raised. When the works council representatives had had a chance to pass on their information to their workmates the general outline of the story was released to the press. By this means rumour was avoided and there was no chance of a worker reading of impending redundancies in the local paper before he had gained first-hand knowledge of it at work. The result was a harmonious working together of management and unions.

By December 1959, amicable talks about the handling of redeployment were going on between management and union officials. Each meeting was minuted and a report printed in the works newspaper. No one was left in ignorance of what was being discussed and at what rate the talks were proceeding. But there was another tough problem, and that was the timing of the announcement of the selection of the fortunate teams who were to operate the electric arc furnaces and the ancillary equipment. A premature announcement might send the men not chosen in search of other jobs while the company needed them to continue working the open hearth shops, perhaps for two or three years more. But Steel, Peech and Tozer reasoned that to hold back this knowledge would be unfair, that men need to know where they stand at such times, so they 'grasped the nettle' and published the lists of names immediately selection was made.

The basis of selection was agreed with the unions and rested on five points: seniority within a working group (melter, teemer, crane driver, etc.); ability; timekeeping record; personal record; and the possession of a certificate from the City and Guilds of London Institute of proficiency in electric steelmaking. This last was only for the melters. There was to be no age limit. Those not chosen were allowed to appeal against the decision.

The age question for retraining was of special interest. The company was not content to set arbitrary age limits based on general assumptions, but sought the opinions of the Professor of Applied Psychology at the University of Sheffield, whose staff undertook to advise on the training organization and chose the methods.

Knowing that the whole span of the project was to be five years, the management also knew that normal wastage would take care of most of the labour surplus over that period, but in order to maintain production they also knew that they would have to continue recruiting manpower to replace retirements and moves. They accordingly introduced the idea of temporary recruitment from January 1960. Anyone joining the company after that month was taken on temporarily only, and they were told this when they applied. Two per cent of applicants refused to come on this basis. To confine eventual redundancies to the ranks of the temporaries the company also decided to reduce the retiring age from 66½ to 65, when men would qualify for both a state and a works pension. The unions readily accepted that earlier retirement was preferable to redundancy for younger men.

Redeployment, which sounds so simple, proved to be very complicated and any brief account such as this oversimplifies it. In the 'fair play' atmosphere generated by the handling of SPEAR it was assumed by all parties that vacancies occurring in other departments should rightfully be offered to the men facing redundancy. A scheme was worked out. Every vacancy was advertised on bulletin boards and in the works paper. Men who were not on the select list were allowed to apply and if successful to move as soon as possible. They were then replaced by temporaries. Five hundred and fifty-four men transferred in this way, and thirty-four others moved to other companies in the group. The company helped with removal costs to places like Scunthorpe and Swindon. One hundred and fifty-one retired, and one hundred and forty left Steel, Peech and Tozer for other employment during this period. Only nine were transferred to other companies by arrangement. Altogether 918 jobs were extinguished one way or another.

For those staying but earning less a compensation formula was devised. It was simple and seemed just, and was accepted. For every pound a week a man's earnings shrank as a result of the reorganization he received a lump sum, tax free, based on his years of service and his age.

Union co-operation was whole-hearted and constant, with daily meetings with the men involved in the changes, so that as nearly as possible everyone was handled individually. As a result of this untiring and meticulous effort not one day was lost in disputes during the period of SPEAR.

A PLANT DIES

THE shutting down of the British Aluminium factory at Milton, Stoke-on-Trent, in 1964 has become an industrial relations classic, recorded in Alan Fox's booklet, which he wrote for the Institute of Personnel Management, *The Milton Plan*. It has been said since that British Aluminium and its managing director at the time, Mr Fred Catherwood, were lucky in having at Milton a history of good labour relations and a particularly intelligent shop stewards' convener. This looks a strange claim to make, given that both the quality of labour relations and the behaviour of the convener are directly the result of managerial attitudes and policy. An intelligent convener can be a thorn in the side of management if he wishes to be.

The Milton shutdown was part of a group rationalization plan. The intention of the group management was to put the Milton work through two other, newer and lower-cost plants at Falkirk and Rheola in South Wales, and abandon the Milton manufacturing unit entirely. An investigating committee working with a management consultant, put up the scheme and it eventually received Board approval. That was in the spring of 1962, and at that stage only the senior management, including the group's personnel manager, were in the know.

The problem was to run down the factory while maintaining an effective labour force at Milton for about fifteen months, the estimated period of the phasing out of the mill, and the taking over of the rolling work by the other units. This meant, among other embarrassments, moving some of the machinery with which Rheola was not equipped. Part of this technical transfer involved rebuilding at Rheola, during which some work would have to go to Milton, so that the doomed factory was suddenly going to have an increase in its activity, followed by a steady diminution. How to accomplish the various stages of such a scheme without taking the workers into the management's confidence and thus risking wholesale premature departures was the heart of the problem. What management feared was that during the stepping up of activity at Milton the works would be vulnerable to a threat of stoppage, which might occur to the more militant workers as a means of pressing the company to change its plans for Milton.

From the first meeting of the investigating committee in spring 1962, only five people knew what was intended. Then, once the decision was taken, the working out of a time-table for announcing the closure was the most important immediate task, beginning with the Board decision on September 5, 1962. It was immediately followed (within a few days) by a meeting with the appropriate national industrial officer of the trade union with most members involved, the National Union of General and Municipal Workers, and another with the branch secretary at Milton. All these talks were held in secret awaiting a general announcement timed for September 14th, when the senior staff would be told first, then the foremen and shop stewards and finally the remaining staff. When these meetings had been held a notice would be posted, having been carefully drafted to avoid ambiguity or vagueness that might look as if the company's stated intentions did not accord with what the press would have to say later. The release of the press announcement was to be 'embargoes' for Monday, September 17th, in the hope that it would receive better treatment, with space for the compensation arrangements and similar details to be reported, and not just a bald paragraph about the closure in Saturday's papers. This meant an anxious week-end, for by that time over a thousand people would know and they were under no obligation to keep quiet about it. The public relations officer decided that the best course was to let the industrial correspondent of the local paper into the secret, explaining about the embargo and then relying on him not to publish a guesswork story that might trigger off all kinds of adverse responses.

A special problem of the Milton labour force was its high age-levels. Out of an hourly-paid force of 840 and a weekly-paid staff of 192 it turned out that more than 700 were over 40, with 150 over 58. A lot of the men had served the company more than twenty years, and some of them even had wives employed at the works as well. Compensation terms had therefore

to be generous and the company set aside a fund of £250,000
for the purpose, out of which payment for transfer to South
Wales would be made. It was probably the high average age
that prevented the successful transfer of more than a handful of
workers to the Rheola plant. This was the one respect in which
the Milton Plan failed. Otherwise the rundown and closure went
off like clockwork. This was in a factory that was not an official
'closed shop' but which had 100 per cent union membership
because of the assiduity of the convener and branch secretary,
a dual role performed by one man who, although on the company's payroll, spent all his time on union affairs.

This dedicated official was the first to hear of the Plan, and
he was very shaken, as was his national industrial officer, who
saw a well-run union branch about to disappear. They were
both worried, too, about the fact that the Plan seemed to be
complete and irreversible by the time it came to their attention. Some members might feel that these two had done less
than their duty. In talks with the group personnel chief the convener came to understand that the closure was inevitable, that
the Plan was designed to alleviate its worst effects on the people
working at Milton, and that industrial action intended to halt
or reverse the Plan would only result in a more precipitate
closure with resultant hardship. Thus was the intelligent convener calmed down. Perhaps British Aluminium were lucky in
him, or perhaps they had behaved so logically and reasonably
throughout that even an obtuse, stupid or antagonistic official
would have come round to their point of view.

Luckily the press on Sunday and Monday gave a favourable
view of the situation, even printing the compensation fund
figure in their headlines in one case. The crucial role of the
press at such a time is admirably illustrated by the Milton
closure. Indeed, well-organized press and public relations
coupled with a history of good labour relations can be seen to
pay off far more than leaving the whole series of events to guesswork and rumour. But, since Milton, large companies have
closed provincial factories far from their London headquarters
with a casualness and indifference amounting in some cases to
harshness. One of British industry's bigger problems is getting
the good examples of industrial behaviour across to the systematic managements who manage everything well but men and
women.

The key role in the management of the Milton Plan was played by a specially appointed, full-time co-ordinator whose duty was to see that the phasing of the transfer to Rheola went without a hitch. But there was some fear among the staff, who were not unionized, that their interest might go by default. They were speedily reassured on this point, but nevertheless a public protest meeting took place in Stoke in November at which M.P.s and local councillors agreed to sending a deputation to the Board of Trade, the purpose of which was to remind the Government of its promises to maintain full employment and to press for the retention of Milton as a manufacturing unit. The President, however, while sympathetic, pointed out that he had no powers to intervene in the affairs of the company.

This flurry of activity, however, underlines the fact that British Aluminium's managers were not having it all their own way. It was in a somewhat hotter mood than had been envisaged in September that negotiations proceeded, having begun in mid-October. There was some soreheadedness about the better treatment meted out to weekly-paid staff as compared with payroll workers and a demand for compensation of a like kind. There was also a grievance about compulsory pensioning off at 55 for women and 60 for men, some of the older employees feeling that they would rather take lump-sum compensation and find other work. A man with thirty years' service was to get £300, while a clerk of similar standing would receive about four times as much. In the end it was agreed to pay full pensions at the ages announced, plus a cash payment, but the staff-works differentials stayed, and were the cause of much bitterness.

It was not till February 1963 that settlements were reached and announced. Meanwhile work went on in the factory at much the same pace as before, but about thirty staff members resigned that month and had to be replaced by temporaries. Looming up was the problem of the lower average rates of pay in Wales as compared with Stoke. Would Milton transferees kick up a fuss if their wage packets were smaller although their cost of living would be smaller too? To get round this an announcement in these terms was made. It cannot have enthused people much to transfer, and indeed the scheme, which had begun in a small way, fizzled out.

The rundown itself had to be based on certain principles. A shortened week was discarded as a possibility because of the consequent drop in earnings and the danger that key skilled workers might leave prematurely for better pay. The first wave of redundancies was confined to men with less than five years' service and with a bad timekeeping record. Then it was to be 'last in, first out' right through the works, excepting for certain special skills, key workers and 'graded' labourers or 'operators'. These were labourers who had achieved some seniority and had three months' experience in a responsible job. Among the women it was agreed that the married ones should leave first. An appeal committee was set up to guard against wrongful inclusion in the redundancy lists. Appeal could also be made against downgrading as the reorganization proceeded.

Oddly, this factory had been through a bad patch and suffered some redundancy ten years earlier, and the experience had alerted both managers and union officials to the sort of dangers that they might encounter. It was the reasonable behaviour of management over the intervening decade that was bearing fruit in 1963. The dismissals and retirements went on throughout the year, culminating in January 1964, when only 341 employees were left. Once these had gone only a care-and-maintenance team remained.

About two weeks before Christmas 1963, a farewell dinner was held at which the convener was presented with his portrait in oils by the general manager-personnel. So Milton came to its end, with dignity and a touch of pathos, but no bones broken.

INDEX

accounting, 17-18, 20, 29, 94, 125-6
Amalgamated Engineering Union, 51, 55, 59, 118, 131
Amalgamated Society of Locomotive Engineers and Firemen, 55
apprenticeship, 12, 22, 39, 133
arbitration, 43, 45, 48ff., 52, 100; board of, 49; court of, 45
Association of Scientific Workers, 53
Association of Supervisory Staffs, Executives and Technicians, (ASSET), 62
Automobile Workers Union, 115

Babbage, Charles, 20
bargaining *see* collective bargaining
bargaining, workplace, 62-4, 67
Bentley, F. R., 86
Bevin, Ernest, 108
bonuses, 20, 85-6, 94, 97, 135
Boulton, James, 19ff., 29
Brech, E. F. L., 19, 22ff., 33
Briggs, Asa, 24
British Aluminium, 141
British Institute of Management, 93, 132
British Railways Board, 55
Brown, Dr. J. A. C., 32, 72, 90, 96
Brown, Professor Phelps, 37
building industry, 41
Burnham Committee, 56
Burns, 79
Burton, F. G., 20

Cadbury, Edward, 24f.
capitalism, 10f., 13, 15, 18, 24, 102f.
car industry, 115-17, 121-2
Catherwood, Fred, 141
change, workers attitude to, 77-88
Chester, T. E., 106
children, employment of, 11, 14-15, 17, 25, 46
Churchill, *Sir* Winston, 41
Civil Service, 49, 56, 103

Clack, Garfield, 121
claims procedure, 50
Clegg, Hugh, 24f., 42, 102-3, 106, 132
Clerical and Administrative Workers' Union, 51
co-partnership, 26, 125
Coal Board, 55
Cole, G. D. H., 102
collective bargaining, 15, 17, 25, 28, 37-47, 53, 57-8, 62-4, 67, 85, 100, 103, 106, 119, 130-6
Combination Laws, 39f.
Committee on the Relations between Employers and Employed, 45
Companies Act (1862), 13, 29
compensation, 139-40, 142-3
conciliation, 43, 48f., 52, 55
Conciliation Act (1896), 44, 48
Conditions of Employment and National Arbitration Order, 70
Confederation of Shipbuilding and Engineering Unions, 51f.
Contracts of Employment Act (1963), 112
cottage industries, 11
courts of inquiry, 44, 49
craft industries, 38, 82
craftsmen, 11, 16, 40

Delafons, Alan, 83
demarcation disputes, 82, 112f., 118, 132-3
democracy, industrial, 27, 92, 100-6
directors, 14, 27, 29, 31, 87, 92, 105, 126
discipline, 9f., 17, 21, 29, 31, 101f., 106, 128
disputes, 48f., 52f., 63, 77, 112f., 116-17, 122, 140; definition of, 49; *see also* strikes
docks, 30, 40f., 50
Draughtsmen's and Allied Trades Association (DATA), 51, 53
Drucker, Peter, 71f.